Debating Capitalism

Debating Ethics

General Editor
Christopher Heath Wellman
Washington University of St. Louis

Debating Ethics is a series of volumes in which leading scholars defend opposing views on timely ethical questions and core theoretical issues in contemporary moral, political, and legal philosophy.

Recently published in the series

Debating Pornography
Andrew Altman and Lori Watson

Debating Education
Is There a Role for Markets?
Harry Brighouse and David Schmidtz

Debating Sex Work
Lori Watson and Jessica Flanigan

Debating Targeted Killing
Counter-Terrorism or Extrajudicial Execution?
Tamar Meisels and Jeremy Waldron

Debating Democracy
Do We Need More or Less?
Jason Brennan and Hélène Landemore

Debating Multiculturalism
Should There be Minority Rights?
Patti Tamara Lenard and Peter Balint

Debating Capitalism

Market Liberalism or Social Democracy

Richard J. Arneson and Jason Brennan

OXFORD
UNIVERSITY PRESS

OXFORD
UNIVERSITY PRESS

Oxford University Press is a department of the University of Oxford. It furthers the University's objective of excellence in research, scholarship, and education by publishing worldwide. Oxford is a registered trade mark of Oxford University Press in the UK and in certain other countries.

Published in the United States of America by Oxford University Press
198 Madison Avenue, New York, NY 10016, United States of America.

Library of Congress Control Number is on file at the Library of Congress

ISBN 9780190076436 (pbk.)
ISBN 9780190076429 (hbk.)

DOI: 10.1093/9780190076467.001.0001

Paperback printed by Marquis Book Printing, Canada
Hardback printed by Lightning Source, Inc., United States of America

The manufacturer's authorized representative in the EU for product safety is Oxford University Press España S.A. of Parque Empresarial San Fernando de Henares, Avenida de Castilla, 2 – 28830 Madrid (www.oup.es/en or product.safety@oup.com). OUP España S.A. also acts as importer into Spain of products made by the manufacturer.

MIX
Paper | Supporting responsible forestry
FSC® C103567
FSC
www.fsc.org

Contents

Figures and Tables

Figures

Tables

PART I

INTRODUCTION BY BRENNAN

Introduction

Which Form of Capitalism Is Best?

Moving Beyond the Socialism vs. Capitalism Debate

The second half of the twentieth century witnessed a prolonged debate about whether capitalism or socialism was most efficient and just.[1] It was also a real-life social scientific experiment run over billions of people in over a hundred countries. By the end of the twentieth century, it seemed the results were in and the debate over.

Capitalism won. The countries that tried different forms of capitalism, such as Australia, Switzerland, the former West Germany, Singapore, Hong King, South Korea, Denmark, and Sweden, got rich and richer. The countries that tried forms of socialism, such as the USSR, the former East Germany, North Korea, Cuba, and China, remained poor.

Despite what Karl Marx might have predicted, the capitalist countries served their relatively "poor" better than the socialist countries managed to serve their middle classes. The socialist countries weren't even supposed to have upper, middle, and lower classes, but they always did. What we call "poor" in rich countries is still rich compared to everyone else. The United States today considers the "poverty line" for a single adult living alone to be about $16,000. That's not a lot of money, sure. Nevertheless, adjusting for the cost of

[1] By joint decision of the coauthors, this Introduction is solo-authored by Brennan. Arneson endorses it, and generally concurs with its content.

Debating Capitalism. Richard J. Arneson and Jason Brennan, Oxford University Press.
 DOI: 10.1093/9780190076467.003.0002

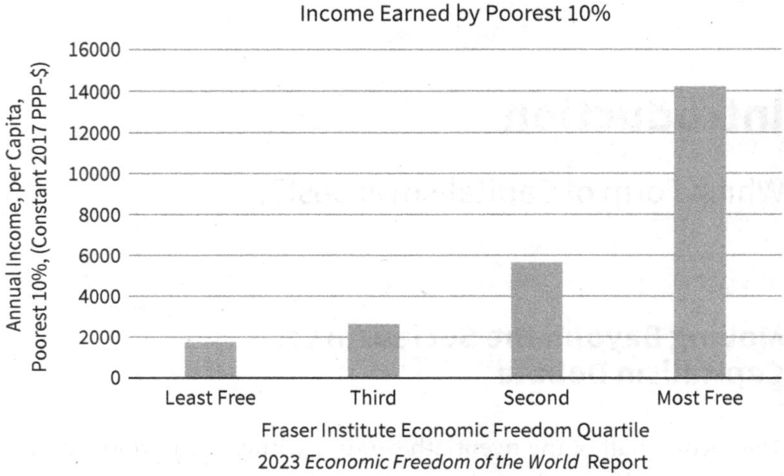

Figure I.1 Income earned by poorest 10%
Source: Gwartney et al. 2023, 19.

living in different places, this "poor American" is still among the top 20–30% of income-earners worldwide and greater than the global *median household* income.[2]

Each year, academic economists working for the Canadian Fraser Institute rate countries according to their commitment to economic freedom, taking account of such factors as access to sound money, free trade, ease of starting and doing business, ease of investing capital, the protection of property rights, and the degree of government control of or manipulation of the economy. The most economically free market countries include Australia, New Zealand, Canada, and Switzerland. Figure I.1 below breaks all countries in quartiles from the most capitalist to the least. It then shows how much real income (that is, adjusted for the local cost of living) people at the 10th percentile of income earn *before* they receive any welfare or social insurance payments from their governments. Notice that the "poor" in the most capitalist countries enjoy significantly higher incomes than their counterparts in the less capitalist countries. To be "poor"

[2] Calculations according to https://www.givingwhatwecan.org/how-rich-am-i, Milanovic (2007), and Flynn (2023).

in a capitalist country means to be significantly richer than the world median per capita income, which as of 2019 is less than $4000 USD.[3]

An ironic indication that capitalism won the debate is what its critics propose as an alternative. Senator Bernie Sanders and Representative Alexandria Ocasio-Cortez claim that we should replace American capitalism with "democratic socialism." When asked to name laudable examples of democratic socialism, Sanders, Ocasio-Cortez, and their supporters point to Sweden, Norway, Denmark, or the Netherlands.

But, as Danish Prime Minister (at the time) Lars Løkke Rasmussen responded to Sanders, "Denmark is far from a socialist planned economy. Denmark is a market economy."[4] Rasmussen's opinion is backed by economists' ratings of how capitalist countries are. In the 2017 Fraser rankings, Denmark was 15th, Finland 17th, the Netherlands 19th, Norway 25th, and Sweden 27th.[5] The Heritage Institute ranks the Netherlands 13th, Denmark 14th, Sweden 19th, Finland 20th, and Norway 26th. More recent rankings move the numbers slightly. Still, the countries some Americans call "socialist" are better described as free market welfare states, in many respects more "free market" than the United States.

We take this as instructive. In this book, instead of debating capitalism vs. socialism, we will debate which *form* of capitalism is best. We'll ask: What is the best expression of a market-based economy, how and in what ways should governments or other institutions intervene, restrict, or supplement market economies to produce the best outcomes for all?

Definitions

What makes a system "capitalist"? We should avoid moralized or pejorative definitions.

[3] Nair (2018) offers $2100 as an estimate. Gallup estimates $2920 as of 2013 (Phelps and Crabtree 2013).

[4] Yglesias (2015).

[5] Gwartney et al. (2017).

What distinguishes economic systems are their background rules and institutions: Who owns what, who makes decisions, and who plans?

We might say a society is capitalist to the extent that it has open markets, with prices and production set by the force of supply and demand, with private ownership of the means of production, with few legal barriers to entry or exit of those markets, and with individuals having a right to trade with others by mutual consent. A society is capitalist to the extent that individuals can own productive property, such as factories or machines.

In contrast, people often define "socialism" as the collective ownership of the means of production. But this distinction misleads. In capitalism, most large companies are collectively owned by stockholders, including owners of mutual funds. In real-life socialist societies, the state, not the people, owns the means of production. The people usually get little say.

We will instead use an operationalized definition of the sort economists use. For instance, the Fraser Institute scores countries' "economic freedom" based upon a combination of the following traits[6]:

1. The "Size" of Government (more government means less capitalist)
   - A system is judged more capitalist (or economically free) to the extent that the government is small, that it avoids owning or maintaining heavy public investments in enterprises, that it consumes low portions of GDP, and that it has low taxes.
2. The Legal System and Property Rights
   - A system is judged more capitalist to the extent that it has strong protection of private property rights, impartial courts and a fair judicial system marked by the rule of law, strong and impartial legal enforcement of contracts, and low interference in the law by the military.
3. Sound Money

[6] Gwartney et al. (2017, 4).

    - A system is judged capitalist to the extent that the central government and bank avoid heavy inflation and manipulation of currency and money markets for political ends, to the extent that central banks are free from political control, and the extent to which citizens are free to own and trade foreign currency.
4. Freedom to Trade Internationally
    - A system is judged capitalist to the extent that it lacks tariffs, regulatory trade barriers, has low costs of importing and exporting, has low black-market exchange rates, and low controls from government on the freedom of goods or people to cross borders.
5. Degree of Regulation
    - A system is judged capitalist to the extent that it lacks regulations on banking, the labor market, and business, including controls on prices, costs of starting businesses, ease of hiring and firing, and costs of overall compliance with regulations.

The Fraser Institute annually scores every country on a 1–10 scale on each of these aspects. It then produces an overall weighted average. A score of 10 indicates a completely free market/capitalist.

In the 2018 ratings, Singapore, New Zealand, Ireland, and Switzerland get overall scores between 8 and 9. Denmark receives a 7.77 overall, with scores above 8 for freedom from regulation, protection of private property, and freedom to trade, and scores near 10 for low regulations in hiring and firing and freedom from credit market regulation. Again, pace Sanders, Denmark is a free market welfare state rather than a socialist country. Denmark combines a free market, lightly regulated capitalist economy with governmental social insurance and redistribution.

The Heritage Institute (working with the *Wall Street Journal*) issues a similar index and uses a similar operationalized definition. A system is judged to be capitalist to the extent that it has the rule of law (judged by strong protection of private property rights, judicial effectiveness, and government integrity), small government size (judged by tax burden, government spending, and fiscal health), regulatory efficiency (judged by business freedom, lower regulation of labor, and monetary freedom), and market openness (judged by trade freedom, investment freedom, and financial freedom).[7]

In the 2019 Heritage Institute, six countries—Hong Kong, Singapore, New Zealand, Switzerland, Australia, and Ireland—are rated as "free." The major social democracies, such as Germany, the United States, Canada, Sweden, the Netherlands, Norway, Finland, Luxembourg, Japan, South Korea, and Iceland, are rated as mostly free, with scores above 7.0 on a 0.0–10.0 scale.

Still, no country receives a 10 or a 1. Every real country has some mix of private commercial markets and government control, regulation, and supplementation of the market. The countries we suspect our readers would prefer to live in, or which they are likely to point to as success stories, generally have scores between a 7.5 and 9.

A Brief Economic History of the World

Throughout most of human history, nearly everyone lived in what we would today consider "extreme poverty." Economist Brad Delong estimates that in 5000 BC, per capita world product—the total amount of yearly economic production worldwide per person—was only about $130 (in 2002 USD), and barely doubled by 1800 to $250.[8] Economist Angus Maddison offers higher numbers: $457 USD (1990 dollars) in 1 AD, rising to $712 USD in 1820.[9] Extreme poverty was once widespread and normal, but now it's not.

In Figure I.2 below, we chart GDP/capita, that is, the total amount of economic production per person in constant, cost-of-living-adjusted 1990 US dollars. We condensed the period from 1 to 1500 AD (and all of history before that) because before 1500, the lines hardly move.

[7] Miller, Kim, and Robert (2019, 9–13).
[8] DeLong (2002, 120).
[9] Maddison (2007, 70); the Maddison-Project, http://www.ggdc.net/maddison/maddison-project/home.htm, 2013 version.

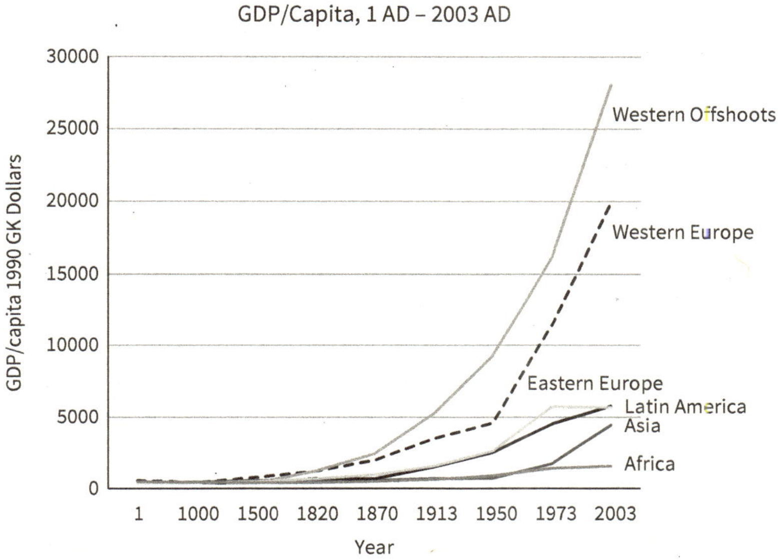

Figure I.2 GDP/capita, 1 AD–2003 AD
Source: Data from Maddison 2007, 70.

In the past 200 years, per capita world product has increased by a factor of at least 35.[10] Absolute levels of wealth grew faster than the population at large. People—and entire countries—got richer.

An American at what the US poverty line today enjoys a standard of living three times higher than the *average* American of 1900.[11] Economist Paul Krugman wrote in 1996, ". . . most families in 1950 had a material standard of living no better than that of today's poor or near-poor . . . .it does not seem at all absurd to say that the material standard of living of the poverty-level family in 1996 is as good as or better than that of the median family in 1950."[12] What we call poor today was considered wealthy 150 years ago.

[10] According to the CIA World Factbook, world per capita income as of 2017 is approximately $17,300 in 2014 US dollars, up from under $500 in 1800.

[11] I use Angus Maddison's historical GDP/capita data, available here: http://www.ggdc.net/maddison/Maddison.htm. See also Maddison (2003).

[12] Krugman (1996).

The wealth we enjoy today did not exist 50 years ago, let alone centuries ago. The United States by itself in 2019 produced something like twice the entire world's economic output in 1950, and 80 times the entire world's economic output in 1000 AD.[13] Wealth has been *made*, not just moved around.

Capitalist Countries Are Rich and Non-Capitalist Countries Are Poor

Growth did not occur equally everywhere. Why not?

In 1821, the gap between Western Europe and the world average was only about 2 to 1, while the gap between the richest and poorest countries was only about 5 to 1.[14] Go back further and the gap closes. In 1000 AD, every person in every geographic region had roughly the same (poor) standard of living.[15]

If the West had gotten rich at the same rate the others grew poor, this would suggest the West grew rich at the expense of the rest, and that wealth was simply moved around, like in a poker game. But we don't see that. We see *real growth*, not merely a reallocation or redistribution of a fixed rate of income. The West grew richer much *faster*, but the rest grew richer too. Every place has more, but some places have much, much more. So, what explains the changes?

Laypeople often presume rich countries have good natural resources while poor countries have poor resources. It's a popular but

[13] Schmidtz and Brennan (2010, 122) and http://www.ggdc.net/maddison/Maddison.htm.

[14] Maddison-Project, http://www.ggdc.net/maddison/maddison-project/home.htm, 2013 version; Landes (1999, 15–25).

[15] As economist Angus Maddison summarizes the trends (Maddison 2007, 70–1):

> In the year 1000 the inter-regional spread was very narrow indeed. By 2003 all regions had increased their incomes, but there was an 18:1 gap between the richest and poorest region, and a much wider inter-country spread.
>
> One can also see the divergence between the "west" (western Europe, US, Canada, Australia, New Zealand) and the rest of the world economy. Real per capita income in the west increased 2.8-fold between the year 1000 and 1820, and 20-fold from 1820 to 2003. In the rest of the world income rose much more slowly—slightly more than a quarter from 1000 to 1820 and seven-fold since then.

puzzling theory. After all, "natural resources" have been around forever, but growth didn't start until recently.

At any rate, economists have rigorously investigated the resource theory and concluded it doesn't explain growth. As economist David Weil summarizes the empirical literature in his widely used textbook *Economic Growth*, "the effect of natural resources on income is weak at best."[16]

Contrary to the thesis, more resource-rich countries often do worse than the resource-poor countries. China has fabulous natural resources. Yet after the 1950s it was and remains poorer (in per capita income and other standard measures) than Singapore or Hong Kong, though the latter have no natural resources. The USSR had better natural resources than the United States, but the United States had a much higher standard of living (including among its poorer classes) than the USSR throughout the Cold War. When Adam Smith wrote the *Wealth of Nations*, the Netherlands and England were significantly richer than France, though France had far better natural resources. And so on.

Indeed, an abundance of natural resources often *inhibits* growth. Economists call this the "resource curse": countries with a high concentration of easily extractable natural resources frequently suffer from economic stagnation, in part because when a country enjoys abundant resources, this encourages governments to act in exploitative and destructive ways.[17]

A second popular view holds that that rich countries are rich because they stole resources and wealth from the rest of the world. For instance, political theorist Seyla Benhabib says she doubts "whether early capitalist accumulation in the West could have been conceivable without colonial expansion."[18]

But, pace Benhabib, this issue is well-researched and she should doubt it. After the 1500s, European countries indeed conquered

[16] Weil (2013, 453).
[17] Weil (2013, 450–1).
[18] Benhabib (2004, 100).

and stole resources from other countries. Does this explain why European countries are rich?

The graph above already casts doubt. If Europe's gains were just everyone's losses, we'd expect to see Europe get rich at the rate the others become worse off. That's not what we see. Perhaps, one might speculate, Europeans were just better at extracting unused resources.

There are bigger problems with the colonial theory. For most of the imperial expansion period, Spain had the biggest empire, but it remained poorer than England or the United Kingdom. Why didn't Russia's enormous empire—full of natural resources—make Russia rich? The United States and Germany got rich *first* and *then* acquired empires. Switzerland got rich without having any empire. After World War II, Singapore, Hong Kong, Macau, and South Korea became rich, but they had no empires. Japan had an empire in the late 1800s through World War II, but it didn't become rich until after it lost the war and its empire. The British conquered and expropriated resources from the Irish, but Ireland quadrupled its GDP/capita between 1970 and today, and is now much richer than the United Kingdom on a per capita basis. After World War II, South Korea got rich and North Korea didn't, even though neither had empires, and even though the latter started with better overall resources plus a larger industrial capacity left over from before the division.

It's also not like Europeans invented extractive imperialism in 1492. If extractive imperialism were the secret to growth, why didn't the Mongol, Qing, Abbisad, Umayyad, Brazilian, Roman, Macedonian, Ottoman, Tibetan, Persian, Aztec, or countless other gigantic empires in the Americas, Europe, Asia, or Africa lead to explosive growth even earlier?

Adam Smith already answered these questions in the *Wealth of Nations*. Smith carefully surveyed the economic value of the goods Britain and other countries had extracted from the Americas and elsewhere, and then compared that to the costs these countries incurred to create and maintain those empires.[19] Smith concluded

[19] Smith (1776, V.3.92).

that these empires *lost* money on net. Yes, they were robbing the rest of the world, but the imperialist countries spent more money on the robbery than the value of the goods they received in return. Smith found that a minority of politically well-connected people—the ones who make the rules—benefitted from the empire, but the majority of British subjects—the ones who had to pay taxes to support the empire—*lost* money on net. The losers lost more than the winners won. Further, Smith showed, imperialism distorted the economy (by encouraging inefficient production methods) and so further hurt Britain and other imperial powers. Britain was getting richer despite its empire, not because of it.

Recent work in economics corroborates Smith's argument. Generally, economists find that empires do not pay for themselves, even when we focus narrowly on the economic interests of imperial powers and ignore the harms to the conquered.[20] By analogy, the Iraq War may have enriched Halliburton and General Dynamics, but most Americans are stuck paying trillions in taxes with no obvious compensating economic benefit.

Instead, the dominant view in mainstream economics is that sustained economic growth resulted and continues to result from having the right economic and political institutions.[21] As economist Dani Rodrik and his coauthors summarize, when it comes to explaining economic growth and why some countries are rich and others poor, "the quality of institutions trumps everything else."[22]

Which institutions produce growth? Countries with (A) robust systems of private property and (B) open markets, (C) protected by the rule of law enforced by (D) stable and inclusive governments, offer much better prospects for significant and sustained

[20] Landes (1999, 423), Davis and Huttenback (1982, 1987), Rosenberg and Birdzell (1986), Kimura (1999), O'Brien (1988), Offer (1993), Ferguson (2003), Edelstein (1982), Foreman-Peck (1989), Coelho (1973), McDonald (2009), and Fieldhouse (1961).

[21] Acemoglu and Robinson (2005, 2013), Cowen and Tabarrok (2010, 92–106), North (1990, 3), North, Wallis, and Weingast (2012), Rodrik, Subramanian, and Trebbi (2014).

[22] Rodrik, Subramanian, and Trebbi (2004: 349–76). Similarly, Cowen and Tabarrok (2010, 101) summarize, "the key to producing and organizing the factors of production [in ways that lead to prosperity] are *institutions* that create appropriate *incentives*."

development than those that lack such institutions.[23] The countries with institutions A–D, such as Switzerland, Canada, Singapore, or Hong Kong, are nearly always rich; the countries that lack A–D are nearly always poor.

As Daron Acemoglu and James Robinson argue, the main difference between good and bad institutions concerns the degree to which they foster extractive activity or instead encourage cooperation and productivity. What they call *inclusive* institutions, such as open markets and strong protections for private property, empower people across society, incentivize them to accumulate capital and use resources productively, and thus tend to benefit all. They give people a stake in and ability to invest long term and engage in mutually beneficial capital accumulation. By contrast, *extractive* institutions—such as dictatorships where the government owns the natural resources, or overly regulated economies where rent seekers rig the rules—empower only some, and thus tend to benefit only small groups of people at others' expense.

Our Debate

We the authors have many disagreements about fundamental matters in political philosophy. For instance, Brennan thinks that people have a fundamental right to economic liberty, even if it didn't produce the best consequences, whereas Arneson does not. Brennan thinks economic equality has no intrinsic value; Arneson does.

However, we are not here planning to examine those fundamentals, in part because others have done so, and in part because we want to debate something more particular and more interesting. "What about the poor or the worst off?" remains one of the fundamental questions people have about capitalism. So, we want to consider which form of capitalism best answers this question.

[23] Acemoglu and Robinson (2005, 2013), Acemoglu, Johnson, and Robinson (2001, 2012), Hall and Jones (1999), Hall and Robert Lawson (2014), and de Soto (2000).

Brennan endorses what can be called "open border capitalism." He defends a world order in which each individual nation has a capitalist economy, but has also eliminated all or nearly all restrictions on who may enter or leave. In this world, people would have the same legal right to move among countries as citizens have to move inside their current country. Brennan argues that this system would far better serve the world's worst-off people than our current system of mostly closed-border welfare states, which he claims mostly redistribute income from the extremely rich to the people who are, by world standards, quite rich and privileged.

Arneson instead defends "social democratic capitalism," which envisions a world in which each nation has, to the extent that its wealth allows, an economic system like that found in the very generous welfare systems of the Nordic social democracies. The Nordic states would assist impoverished ones in establishing social democratic institutions, which would then drive domestic economic growth and raise the quality of life of the population. In such a world, rich countries would have significant obligations to assist the economic development and boost the prosperity of poor countries. Allowing increased immigration might well help fulfill these obligations. But these obligations to the global poor, even if extremely demanding, could be fulfilled even by countries that close their borders to would-be migrants.[24]

[24] Thanks to an anonymous referee for suggesting we make it clear what our main debate will be here.

PART II
ARNESON

1
Overview

For several decades, the regimes called "social democratic" in Scandinavian countries have stood out as a beacon of hope to those who envisage progress as combining capitalism and equality. In a capitalist economy, production is for the most part organized around privately owned firms selling goods and services to customers in a market in which people are free to make deals on mutually agreed terms. These terms might over time give rise to almost any degree of inequality depending on circumstances, but in some European societies, most decisively and stably in Sweden, Norway, Denmark, and Finland (often grouped together with Iceland), a democratic state has regulated and coordinated economic outcomes, bringing about more equality, in ways that matter, across citizens. Now in the third decade of the twenty-first century, these social democratic regimes are altering and perhaps losing their strong egalitarian tilt (Jensen 2023, 60), although earlier predictions of their demise have proved premature (Lindbeck 1997). The title of a 2016 academic book (Schall) has proclaimed "the rise and fall of the miraculous welfare machine" in Sweden.

However, whether these social democratic regimes rise again or fall would not gainsay their achievements in their prime. It is a mistake to imagine that if we could just get the morally right institutions in place, they would last forever. There is not necessarily any ratchet effect that blocks backsliding from justice. Our human nature is not saintly. We should be seeking to bring about as much social justice as we can over the long run.

In this chapter, Nordic social democracy (NSD) refers to the main features of the institutions and practices of the four countries

Debating Capitalism. Richard J. Arneson and Jason Brennan, Oxford University Press.
 DOI: 10.1093/9780190076467.003.0004

named above—political democracy and a well-functioning capitalist economy, incorporating centralized wage bargaining, along with generous welfare state policies. In these countries, democratic voting initiates and sustains a high level of taxation, high levels of government spending on social programs, and moreover, social spending that is generous to the poor.

In the pages that follow I shall contrast the institutions and performance of NSD with those of two other rich country regime types—(1) countries with governments that have significantly lower taxes than the Nordics and significantly lower public spending on programs to benefit the poor and (2) countries in Southern Europe and to some extent central Europe that are also called social democratic and have high taxes but which have policies that favor a male breadwinner family structure and also insiders including public employees and the elderly and that do less for outsiders including the poor. The United States is the most prominent example of a type 1 regime. The United Kingdom, Canada, and Australia are somewhat in this mold. Italy most clearly exemplifies the type 2 regime. This chapter argues for the superiority of NSD over the more laissez-faire type 1 and the socially conservative type 2 models.

What Are the Egalitarian Achievements of NSD?

Less inequality in disposable money income and in publicly provided goods and services

The pretty much uncontroversial starting point is that the Nordic countries exhibit certain features that mark them off as different from other wealthy countries around the world. They are more egalitarian in several ways. First, in money terms. The distribution of disposable income across the citizens of the country is more equal in the Nordics than elsewhere. That is to say, the gap between the incomes of those at the top of the income distribution (90th percentile) and those in the middle (50th percentile) is less, and the gap between the middle and those near the bottom (10th percentile) is also less. Your yearly disposable income is your income from all sources, subtracting the taxes you pay and adding any money distributed to you by the state.

To be sure, by comparison, income per capita and so Gross Domestic Product (GDP) per capita are higher in the United States than in the Nordic countries. But this difference is fully accounted for by the fact that Americans aged 25–64 on average work between 150 and 300 hours more per year at paid employment than do citizens of Nordic countries aged 25–64. Productivity (GDP per hour of work) is just as high in the Nordics (except Finland) as in the United States.

The lesser inequality of post-tax post-transfer incomes in the Nordic countries than in the United States is not only, or even primarily, the result of government's more aggressive taxation and transfer policies in these countries. The pre-tax pre-transfer income of prime-age adults is also less unequal there than in the United States. Over the 1975–2010 period, Norway and Sweden, the Nordic nations with least pre-tax income inequality and most generous welfare state programs, were twice as generous in welfare state tax-and-transfer as the United States and had only one-half of the pre-tax income inequality of the United States. In 2019, the Gini measure of inequality in disposable incomes for those aged 18–64 in the countries of Sweden, Denmark, Finland, and Norway averaged together was 0.27 and in market income before redistribution was 0.39; the comparable figures are 0.36 and 0.45 for the United Kingdom and for the United States, a whopping 0.39 and 0.47 (Mogstad et al. 2025). The Gini coefficient is a measure of inequality ranging from zero (no inequality) to one (one individual in the population has all). The lower the score, the smaller the amount of transfer that would have to take place to move from the actual present level of inequality to none.

The Nordic countries feature tax-funded public provision of health care, education (through college for those qualifying for college admission), disability compensation, and subsidized day care for children and parental leave following childbirth, universally for all citizens in need of these services. Unemployment compensation payout is larger, up to a point, the larger your income, and old age pensions vary with income and years of employment, and so the amount of contribution made to the pension fund when employed. Taxation of labor income is mildly progressive (as your income rises, your tax rate increases), and the social insurance payouts for unemployment, disability, and pensions, along with the child care subsidy, are more generous to lower earners, so have a redistributive component. If I am a low earner, then insofar as public provision covers some of my basic needs, tilting in favor of those like me who are less well off, the disposable income I end up with has enhanced value, giving me more freedom to choose to pursue whatever I might choose to seek.

Equality Between Men and Women

In every country in the world, throughout recorded history to the present, the social opportunities and life prospects of men and women have been unequal, with women getting the short end of the stick. (To be sure, women on average live longer than men, but presently on average men and women enjoy about the same number of years of healthy life free of disabling conditions, and women in developed countries report being in bad health more than do men.) For several decades now, the Nordic countries have been leaders in making progress toward equality for women by available measures.

Labor force participation rates for women aged 25–54 have been significantly higher in Denmark and Sweden than in the United States during the entire span of years from 1970 to 2023 (Goldin 2025). Here the conservative social democratic states of Southern Europe (Italy, Spain, and Greece) follow a different pattern. There the model is a male breadwinner and female homemaker. The labor force participation rates of women (the percentage of women employed or seeking work) are 80% in Sweden and 75% in Denmark, compared to 55% in Italy. The employment rates of women show a similar divergence between the Nordics and Southern Europe.

Having a paying job or self-employment gives you more independence. If you are partnered with a man, as many heterosexual women are, gaining an income on your own tends to give you more bargaining power in your relationship with your partner. If you have children, sticking with your job and career arguably maintains your independence and also sustains the opportunities for fulfilling achievements that jobs and careers can offer. The Nordic countries lead in providing paid parental leave after childbirth (a portion going to the father), along with subsidized and affordable pre-school child care plus after-school care for children of school age, all of which make it easier for mothers to sustain paid employment. Putting these policies in place, these countries pursue a feminist agenda.

If you are a woman and employed, what pay will you earn, compared to employed men? The unadjusted gender wage gap is defined as the difference between the median earnings of men and of women aged 25–64 and employed full-time, expressed as a percentage of the median earnings of these men. In countries where the labor force participation rate for women is low, this gender wage gap also tends to be low, since in these countries, highly qualified women are much more likely to be employed than those less qualified. In OECD (mostly economically developed, wealthy) countries, in 2021, this gender wage gap was just under 5% in Norway and Denmark, 7.5% in Sweden, 9% in Italy, about 17% in the United States and Canada, and slightly less than 17% in Finland (OECD 2023). (By contrast, the comparable figure for South Korea is over 30, for Israel and Latvia about 24, and for Japan about 22.5.)

When a country largely conforms to the male breadwinner model, husbands mainly do paid labor and paying self-employment, and women are occupied in childrearing and housework. For any given couple, with particular preferences, there might be any of many unequal splits of paying labor, childrearing, and housework that would be better for both individuals than an equal split. But if women were not pressured by social norms to go only for homemaking (and men to be the family boss), we might expect that overall for the ensemble of men and women in partnerships, one would see in aggregate an equal split of these activities across men and women. Social arrangements and social norms should not push women away from leaving the home and contributing to the public sphere. Here too, the Nordics lead the way, though only partway so far, toward a world in which men and women mix it up on equal terms in market economy roles and if raising a family together, share home tasks fairly. The expectation is that this would show up as a statistical equal split.

In light of this goal, it is noteworthy that the number of extra hours per week that wives on average between 2009 and 2019 expended in unpaid childrearing and housework chores compared to their husbands was 3 in Italy, 2.7 in Greece, 1.75 in the United States, but only 0.8 in Sweden, and 0.9 in Denmark.

How single-parent heads of households in different countries fare is another indicator of the degree to which a society is achieving equal life prospects for women, since about 85% of these single parents are women. Over the period 1978 to 2008, the poverty rate among single-parent households ranged from 17% to 7% in Norway, 11% to 5% in Sweden and Denmark, and from 5% to 13% in Finland. In 2008, this poverty rate was about 8% in Denmark, 9% in Sweden, 10% in Norway, and 12% in Finland. By comparison, in the United States over this period, 35% to 40% of households headed by a single parent were in poverty, and about 38% in 2008. The Southern European countries of Spain and Italy recorded percentages of single-parent poverty midway between the Nordics and the United States; Greece in 2008 performed better, with a 12% rate in 2008 (Maldonado and Niewenhuis 2014).

In the 2023 Gender Equality Index reported by the European Institute for Gender Equality, Sweden ranked first, followed by the Netherlands and then Denmark, with Finland in eighth place, well above the EU average. Of the Southern European social democracies, only Spain (in fourth place) scored above the EU average; Italy, Portugal, and Greece all fell below that. The 2020 Global Gender Gap Report issued by the World Economic Forum ranked countries by an overall measure of their gender gaps between men and women in the areas of economic participation and opportunities, educational attainment, health and survival, and political empowerment. The four countries with overall least gender gaps were Iceland,

Norway, Finland, and Sweden. Its rankings for 2018 show the same four countries top-ranked.

A Women, Peace, and Security Index issuing from an institute at Georgetown University registers country by country data in the areas of inclusion (women's attainments in education, employment, and parliamentary representation, as well as access to cell phones and financial services), justice (including absence of legal discrimination against women, access to justice, maternal mortality, and bias in favor of sons), and security (intimate partner violence, political violence targeting women, perceptions of community safety, and the share of women who live in close proximity to armed conflict). In 2023, the index core of Denmark was the highest, followed by Switzerland and Sweden. Tied for fourth place were Finland, Luxembourg, and Iceland. Next ranked was Norway. The United Kingdom ranked #26, the United States #37. Of the conservative Southern European social democracies, Portugal ranked #17, Spain ranked #27, Italy #34, and Greece #51.

Equality and fairness between young and old

Unfairness to children has long-term reverberations. Being shortchanged when you are very young can impede your development of the character traits and skills that you need to thrive throughout life, as well as to be able and disposed to play fair with others.

In 2014, a European Union study of households reporting inability to afford 17 basic items for children such as some new clothes, two pairs of properly fitting shoes, fruits and vegetables daily, protein daily, books suitable for children, and holidays showed least child deprivation in Sweden, Denmark, Finland, and Iceland along with Luxembourg, Slovenia, and Switzerland. Greece and Portugal showed high prevalence of child deprivation, and Italy, Spain, and the United Kingdom showed a medium to high level. (Norway is not in the European Union but in other studies shows up as similar to the other Nordics in child deprivation prevalence.)

An important and difficult age group fairness issue involves the share of public spending that should flow to children compared to the share that goes to adults. A particular concern is spending on children that is in effect insurance against the sheer bad luck of having resource-poor, inept, or ill-motivated parents or parent-substitutes, or even worse, none at all.

Nordic policies help here. One example is the reform of old age pensions so that they do not come to eat up the public spending budget when the share of the population that is elderly is increasing (Lindert 2021). Another example is their providing equal per pupil funding for the public primary and secondary schools that almost all children attend. But social scientists remind us that this is insufficient to provide equal educational opportunities for all, as some parents (especially educated parents) sort themselves by relocating so their children attend schools with more stimulating peer children and better teachers. Better teachers sort themselves into better schools where the students are more stimulating and less difficult to teach. Sources of inequality run deep (for Denmark, see Landerso and Heckman 2017).

The Nordic countries have business-friendly regulatory environments, which result in greater freedom for a firm to fire a worker and hence greater willingness to hire new workers, all else equal. The upshot is that it is easier in the Nordics than in many countries—including the United States and also Southern European countries, including Italy, Greece, and Spain, and also some Eastern European countries—for young people entering the labor market to secure a paying job. Since gaining job-related skills and employment experience in early adult life increases one's earnings over the life cycle, this is an important component of fairness to young people in a society. In 2023, in the European Union, the percentage of NEETS (those neither in employment nor education nor training) among people aged 15–29 was second-lowest in Sweden and seventh-lowest in Denmark. Finland was more in the middle of the pack, but still significantly lower than Spain, Greece, especially Italy. Norway and Iceland, not EU members, in 2022 had percentages of NEETS close to those of Sweden.

Other Indicators of Good Quality of Life, and Its Equalization Across Persons, in the Nordics

Labor force participation rates, employment rates, and life expectancy are high in the Nordics, at least compared to the United States. The labor force participation rate is the number of those employed and seeking employment divided by the number of the working-age population. The employment rate is the number of those employed divided by the number of the working-aged population. If having a paying job and living a long life are likely good for a person, then the Nordic countries do well by these indicators of quality of life.

The United Nations has ranked almost all countries in the world according to a Human Development Index. The Index combines life expectancy at birth, average years of education for adults, and average expected years of schooling for children, and gross national income per capita adjusted for purchasing power parity into an overall score. In 2025, based on 2023 data, the top-ranked country was Switzerland, followed by Norway, Iceland, Denmark, and Sweden, ranked second to fifth. Australia ranked seventh. Finland ranked twelfth. The United Kingdom, Canada, New Zealand, and the United States had similar scores below Finland's. Spain ranked 28th, Italy 30th, Greece 34th, and Portugal 40th.

A privately run Legatum Prosperity Index ranks almost all countries of the world by amalgamating scores on variables grouped under the headings of economic quality, business environment, governance, education, health, safety and security, personal freedom, social capital, and natural environment. The 2023 Legatum Prosperity Index ranks Denmark first, followed by Sweden, Norway, and Finland. Three central European welfare states rank fourth to sixth. Among low-tax high-inequality states, the United Kingdom ranks 12th, Canada 13th, and Australia 15th. The United States ranks 19th. Spain, Italy, and Greece are respectively in places #24, #30, and #40.

Right-Wing Objections to NSD and Left-Wing Responses

To call these egalitarian outcomes achievements is to assume they are desirable, and to call them social justice achievements assumes they are required by legitimately enforceable moral principles. To put it mildly, not everyone agrees.

The economist Paul Krugman published an op-ed column deriding American right-wingers for claiming that moderate Democrats in US politics nowadays aspire to turn their country into a "socialist hellhole, like Denmark" (Krugman 2018). What planet are these right-wingers living on? Denmark is a political democracy with strong welfare state institutions and policies. It bears no resemblance whatsoever to the socialism of Stalin, Mao, Fidel Castro, or Hugo Chavez. How could it make any sense to blur the huge gap between (1) a command economy of state ownership ruled by a one-party state and (2) a market economy based on private ownership and paired with a democratic state committed to civil liberties and also to policies aimed at ensuring that the benefits of economic prosperity are widely shared across members of society?

But this rhetorical question itself blurs some important distinctions. From a certain perspective, socialists and social democrats are birds of a feather, alike in ways that render both objectionable for the same reasons. The right-winger (e.g., Nozick 1974) starts with the surmise that those who favor a command economy and those who favor the social democratic market economy as implemented in Scandinavian countries are both reasoning from similar egalitarian principles and just disagree about what are the best means to fulfill these principles in present circumstances. Moreover, clearly and obviously, these shared principles are bad and immoral, from their perspective.

These egalitarian principles imply, for example, that it is OK for the government to be messing with the outcomes of a well-functioning capitalist market economy by redistributing from winners to losers. Such government action is unacceptable, the right-winger objects. Redistribution rewards the unproductive and punishes the productive, which ends up making us all worse off. Doing that also tends to encourage the vices of laziness and dependence and discourage the virtues of self-reliance and willingness to work hard. Moreover, people have property rights to the income and wealth they gain in market exchange by hard work and initiative. And if your parents decide to transfer wealth they have legitimately earned to give their children a leg up, they have a right to transfer what they own as they wish—as does anybody who acquires wealth fairly and squarely. Furthermore, people have a moral right to participate with resources they legitimately own, including their own bodies, in voluntary market exchange and reap the benefits—or suffer the losses.

If you believe these things, you might reasonably believe that a government's wrongly messing with capitalist markets supposedly to help the needy might take the form of expropriating productive property and running the economy by centralized state control. But it could just as well take the form of squeezing people by imposing high taxes and using the funds collected to benefit those it favors. Another way of wrongly messing would involve imposing ham-fisted regulations that bulldoze and distort the economy into a shape the government thinks it prefers. All of these ways of "socializing" the economy are wrong for the same underlying reason: They wrongly violate the rights of each of us to our liberty and property. Notice that the right-winger might uphold strong rights to liberty and property as intrinsically morally correct, specifying what we owe to each other, or alternatively, on the grounds that promoting their fulfillment is an excellent means to bring about wealth and prosperity that benefits us all. Or they might hold that upholding their favored version of rights to liberty and property is both intrinsically morally required and instrumentally beneficial.

Moreover, advocates of socialism and big government characteristically try to justify the measures they favor by appeal to broadly egalitarian principles. It would not be misleading to call these "socialist" principles, harking back to the critiques of unregulated laissez-faire capitalism as it arose in England and Europe in the mid-nineteenth century. The critics then called for socializing the market economy without being clear what institutions would suffice to remedy the problems they identified. They conceivably could end up supporting a full-blown centralized state control of the economy under the rule of a Communist party, as in Cuba or China, or instead supporting a cradle-to-grave nanny state as in social democratic countries including Denmark, Finland, Norway, and Sweden, or instead much more moderate reforms.

So the right-wingers suggesting that American liberals are trying to turn the United States into a "socialist hellhole, like Denmark" were making a clear and simple point. It's that from a right-wing perspective, socialists and social democrats and even fans of twentieth-century Communism are all alike in being tyrannical opponents of liberty and private property as conceived by right-wingers.

Of course, moderate liberals might have no desire to introduce into the United States anything close to NSD, with its generous welfare state policies and egalitarian tilt. They're not committed to strongly egalitarian principles. And egalitarians might strongly support political democracy along with basic civil liberties and firmly reject authoritarianism. The social democrat is not in the same boat with the Communist, so where that latter's boat sails is irrelevant to the assessment of social democracy, including its egalitarian exemplar, NSD.

But if you support the egalitarian features on display in Nordic social democracies, it makes sense to suppose that to justify them, you must appeal to some sort of egalitarian principles that can withstand critical scrutiny and claim our allegiance. Any such principles will oppose the private-ownership-oriented conception of individual liberty that political conservatives celebrate. Call this view that privileges the freedom to own private property "propertarianism."

The "propertarian's" ideal of freedom is being free to do whatever you please with whatever you come to own in a capitalist market economy, so long as you don't harm others in certain familiar ways (force, violence, fraud, theft, imposition of physical harm, and coercion based on threats to do any of the foregoing). This is not the freedom we should prize at the rock-bottom level. You might end up uneducated, unskilled, and penniless, and though formally free to do whatever the laws allow, in fact substantially unfree to do anything at all. As Karl Marx observed almost two centuries ago, negative liberty, consisting of the opportunity to try to do what you choose without others interfering with your attempt, is valuable, but not enough. The freedom that is worth caring about also includes the positive liberty capacity actually to succeed in doing things that are worth caring about.

The propertarian ideal of freedom also sweeps too broadly. Not all freedom is worth protecting. If others are cooperating to provide public goods like police protection and the rule of law that fall on everybody living on a territory independently of their choice, you should not be free to free ride on the cooperative benefits. You should rather be required to contribute your fair share of the costs of provision.

The propertarian ideal of freedom arguably sweeps too broadly in another way. The right-wing objection to the "cradle to the grave nanny state" strongly opposes all paternalism. This is restricting someone's liberty, against her will, for her own good, or in a weaker sense, acting towards a normal competent adult on the basis of doubting that the person will choose competently in some choice she is making. Restricting people against their will for their own good, and expressing doubt in their competence, are often misguided. But not always. This matters for social policy. We are not always good choosers in all domains, and the ability to choose well also varies across persons. Some people are poor choosers through no moral fault of their own. The duty to help everyone live well can require overriding individuals' own judgment, as when a social democratic state offers important help to people in the form of specific benefits like health care and old age pensions, and aids to finding employment rather than simply handing out cash to beneficiaries to spend as they choose.

The propertarian's idea that there is a natural right to own stuff also merits scrutiny. This claim is that each person has a natural right to acquire full ownership over material resources, use them as she sees fit provided she does not thereby cause harm to others in certain limited ways, become richer or poorer by voluntary trades and deals with others, keep for herself whatever she gains, and pass all of it along to her children or others she might happen to favor, and that those who deny this claim are tyrannical opponents of liberty. An opposed view denies that there is ever an unconditional right to ownership; your right to own stuff is conditional on your using what you own to benefit both self and others. More broadly, ownership rules in a society are not fixed by any basic moral right, instead are tools (very useful tools, to be sure) to be assessed by how well they function to promote further fundamental justice goals and adjusted according to proper assessment.

Preview of the Rest of Part II

These challenges against the right-wing position do not suffice to specify, much less justify, egalitarian moral principles. Chapter II.2 describes NSD institutions and objectives. Chapter II.3 explores what can be said for and against equality with a view to identifying plausible egalitarian principles. Two families of principles are identified. Welfarist egalitarianism (WE) says that what we fundamentally morally owe to one another is to maximize a proper balancing of two goals: (1) making the total sum of good quality life enjoyed by persons as large as possible and (2) bringing it about that good quality life is not excessively unequally divided across people. Relational egalitarianism (RE) says that what we fundamentally morally owe to one another is to relate to each other as basic equals, avoiding social hierarchy. Versions of RE abound. A common thread is that all persons should have (1) effective freedom to pursue any life aims they might choose and (2) equal opportunity for political influence in a democratic society.

Chapter II.4 defends NSD institutions and practices by appeal to egalitarian principles, concentrating on WE. The upshot of Chapter II.4 is that if you care about advancing social justice for your countrymen, you would do well to promote NSD-type institutions in your country, or else some alternative mix of institutions and practices that would bring about results that mimic Nordic achievements.

However, this way of framing the question of social justice and how to advance it, though pragmatically useful in a world of independent nation-states whose members mostly care about themselves, is arguably morally off-kilter. In a world marked by huge extremes of wealth and poverty worldwide, with poor people concentrated in poor countries, and the worst off in developed countries almost all better off in life prospects than the average inhabitant of the Earth, justice for our fellow countrymen is not full justice. To measure gains and losses in social justice in a proper accounting, our justice standard should be registering gains and losses in any person's condition anywhere on Earth as counting the same regardless of where on Earth the person happens to live. If justice involves a tilt toward equality, we should be seeking equality worldwide, not equality myopically measured in each separate country taken one by one. If morality demands good lives for people with good life fairly (equally) shared across persons, then morality demands achieving that goal worldwide. If justice demands fulfillment of the moral rights of each person, with priority given to achieving gains for those worse off in this respect, progress toward fulfillment of that goal is measured across all persons, not those in one or another country.

Chapter II.5 explores how, from this global justice perspective, we should assess NSD in the wealthy countries where it exists. Some hold that the global justice obligations of rich countries require that they open up their borders pretty widely to immigration from poor countries. The immigrants would improve their lives, and those left behind in the less developed countries would benefit as well, and current citizens in the ready developed countries, on average, would suffer little or not at all. The catch is that such opening up of national borders would, in practice, be incompatible with maintaining generous welfare state institutions. In short, the claim is that fulfilling global justice obligations conflicts with upholding NSD. In Chapter II.5, I shall argue that this argument misfires. Fulfilling global obligations, to the extent this is feasible, is compatible with maintaining or instituting NSD in rich countries, even if opening borders would result in NSD demise. Moreover, NSD arrangements, tilting toward equality, would be desirable not just in the few Scandinavian countries where they have taken root, and not only in wealthy countries, but anywhere that they can take root.

2
The Institutions and Objectives of Nordic Social Democracy

A social democracy is a democratic political order with a capitalist economy that pursues pro-poor policies. All wealthy democracies do this to some extent, but the United Kingdom, some Asian countries, and especially the United States are outliers, pursuing less redistribution from rich to poor than several European countries. The Scandinavian countries are at the far end of the social democratic scale, doing more than other countries, and stably over several decades, down to the present day.

In this discussion, the term "Nordic social democracy" (NSD) refers to a set of institutions and policies associated with the Scandinavian countries of Sweden, Denmark, and Norway, along with Finland (also to a degree, Iceland). The association is loose: These countries do not have identical institutions and public policies. NSD consists of heterogeneous arrangements, varying across the four Nordic countries, and also varying over time within each country. Given this complexity and variation, what one picks out as core or relegates to periphery is a judgment call. I'll try to be explicit about my reasons for highlighting the features I single out, but readers will be aware that these judgment calls might be made differently.

The Scandinavian countries also vary in their conditions, which affect what policy choices are feasible options for them, and which of the feasible options would be advisable to pursue. For example, Norway differs from the others in having large wealth by way of offshore oil reserves. They also differ in their particular historical

Debating Capitalism. Richard J. Arneson and Jason Brennan, Oxford University Press.
 DOI: 10.1093/9780190076467.003.0005

vicissitudes. For example, Denmark and Norway endured military occupation by German troops during World War II.

Listed below are some core elements of NSD institutions and policies, along with indications of how they differ from other models of capitalist democracy.

A Market Economy Based on Private Ownership, Including Private Ownership of Productive Resources

The hope is that a market economy, regulated to correct for market imperfection and market failure and distributional concerns, can deliver outcomes for people over the long run that will satisfy social justice standards as well as or better than any feasible alternative arrangements.

Nordic social democracy from its beginnings in the 1930s aims at balanced class compromise, not class conflict. The social democratic parties, with a base in labor unions, joined with parties representing smallholding farmers in pushing a common agenda that did not include expropriation of private property in land along with collectivization of agriculture. Nor did the social democratic agenda call for expropriation of the wealth of capitalist property owners (Sejersted 2011). By report, there are more billionaires per capita nowadays in Norway and Sweden than in the United States (Jensen 2021, 47).

Social democracy also accepts, to a degree, private ownership by each individual of productive resources in her own body. Were I to have, for example, enormous singing talent, or sports ability, that could command a very high salary, I could deploy that talent to earn money and become wealthy.

Social democratic acceptance of the market economy framework reflects an acceptance that just as sustained cooperation among us humans requires a state that coerces us by threat of penalties for noncooperation, sustained productive cooperation requires an organization of the economy that gives individuals significant self-interested incentives for voluntarily being of service to others. Our natural dispositions include a capacity for cooperating with others on fair terms, but the design of fair practices and institutions must avoid excessive reliance on our limited and contextually variable capacities for altruistic self-sacrifice.

Political Democracy

Along with being organized as a capitalist market economy, having political democracy does not uniquely characterize social democratic countries, including the Nordic variant. These features are common to a large swath of wealthy nations.

A society's political arrangements are democratic, we shall say, when legislators and top executive branch political officials are chosen by majority rule elections, with each citizen having an equal vote, against a background of wide freedom of speech and freedom of association. Some writers advance a much more demanding standard for characterizing a society as (fully) democratic. On this view, political decisions are made democratically if and only if, and to the degree that, they are made by a process which all citizens have equal opportunity to influence (Kolodny 2023). Opportunities are equal just in case all citizens have equal formal opportunity to influence the political process, and in addition have equal informal opportunities that depend on possession of wealth and leisure time, and other resources. If democracy is interpreted in these demanding terms, varies by degree, and is accorded strict priority over distributive egalitarian objectives (Rawls 1999a), much of what I say in these pages in support of NSD is called into question.

In a study seeking to explain the greater redistribution from rich to poor that one sees in Europe compared to the United States, Alberto Alesina and Edward Glaeser (2004) find that a factor that explains about half of this difference consists in differences in democratic constitutions, especially proportional representation, and including also absence of federalism and checks and balances that disfavor moves from the status quo. Under proportional representation, roughly, the fraction of the electorate that votes for a political party equals the fraction of the seats in the legislature accorded to that political party. So while I treat social democracy as by definition combining "social" policies and democracy, a particular form of democracy may contribute to bringing about the social features that also figure in the term's definition.

High Tax Rates, Yielding a Large Pool of Money to Fund a Big State, But Taxation That Is Close to Proportionate, Not Especially Progressive

According to OECD 2018 statistics, the tax burden as a fraction of GDP is 42.5% on average in Denmark, Sweden, and Norway, and 26.3% in the United States (Jensen 2021).

A tax is proportionate if it takes the same fraction of each taxpayer's income, whether the taxpayer's income is high or low, and progressive, to the degree that those with higher incomes pay an increasingly large fraction of their income.

A feature of NSD is that the tax and transfer system is pro-poor and egalitarian in how tax money is spent, much more than in the procedures by which tax money is collected (Kenworthy 2011, 2020; Lindert 2021, ch. 7). These countries rely heavily on income taxes and on consumption taxes, combined with small taxes on corporate profits. Taxes overall are close to proportionate. The reliance on taxes on consumption is common across European states, probably because the tax is simple to collect and hard to evade.

Having large tax revenues could accompany a small government, which would simply tax and redistribute money. But the Nordic nations have large state sectors, operating public education systems, single-payer health care, and other state-provided services.

Generous Social Insurance Programs

Welfare state policies provide insurance to individuals that cushions the shock of welfare-diminishing life events that befall some individuals and not others. The policies complement or replace private insurance that individuals might purchase (against risks for which private insurance is available). Old age pensions protect individuals against the risk of becoming old without having enough savings to yield income support in old age. Health care plans pay for health care that is needed when one suffers from disease and injury. Unemployment insurance compensates an individual, for a time, who has lost employment.

Savings accrued can cushion individuals against the financial burden of the risks described above, but those who are low in income also tend to lack savings. In this respect, generous social insurance can compensate for small wealth holdings.

Capitalism is often praised for having a casino aspect. One can gamble and perhaps strike it rich. The opportunity to gamble is plausibly regarded as a valuable opportunity, especially when the gambling tends to produce net gains overall for people, and it's not that whenever one wins a certain amount, that same gain is offset by exact same losses overall to others. But capitalism has an unavoidable casino aspect. We are forced by the ensemble of other people's choices to undergo big risks largely beyond our power to control. We reasonably seek some freedom from the resultant insecurity. Richard Layard observes, "If security is what most of us desperately want, it should be a major goal for society. The rich have quite a lot of it and the poor less. A happy society requires a lot of it all round" (Layard 2005). In an economy with increasing reliance on global trade, economic vicissitudes in distant lands can have immediate local impact—another source of economic insecurity.

As already noted, NSD is distinguished from plain social democracy not by having welfare state programs but by their comparative generosity. The programs are generous in handing out a lot of benefits and in providing a higher level of benefits in proportion to national income than is the case in affluent countries other than the Scandinavian ones. Of course, we should be concerned not just with benefit levels but with the amount of good they do over the long run. Some conservatives hold that generous welfare state programs are bad for their recipients. Being assured of a monthly welfare check,

I will lack sufficient incentive to seek and hold paying employment, spend the money in ways that are detrimental to my long-term prospects of living well, and so on. If these claims were generally correct, we should be generally suspicious of generous benefits.

A social insurance program can be generous, handing out a lot of benefits, without being generous to the poor. Southern European opt for these. A government-provided old age pension plan could provide benefits by taking from people in proportion to their income each year and providing income to those living after retirement in proportion to their lifetime earnings. High earners get a lot, low earners a little, those never employed nothing, and those hardly ever employed barely anything. Those with low income and long bouts of unemployment would not be treated generously by such a program. When I describe the NSD social insurance policies as generous, I mean generous to the poor.

It has been remarked that you can have any two of the following but not all three: Low taxes, high initial levels of benefit to the very poor, and no perverse incentives. Faced with this choice, the NSD countries give up low taxes. The perverse incentives alluded to here include incentives to remain a beneficiary of pro-poor aid rather than become self-supporting because the gains from such employment as one can secure are very slight, or even negative taking into account the government-provided benefits one loses by becoming employed. To avoid such perverse incentives, in one way or another benefits to the poor must taper gradually as earned income rises, so a broad swath of people get benefits. There need be nothing on balance undesirable about this effect, but it conflicts with low taxes. Another possibility would be not tapering benefits at all, as would occur if one provided a flat compensation to a person afflicted with a disability, the compensation not being withdrawn if the individual gains income in other ways. But if benefits are provided to a large percentage of the population, going this way also rules out having low taxes.

The poor are those with little money, but we are using lack of money here as a rough proxy for disadvantage—afflictions in themselves that make your life go worse for you. Notice that insofar as programs take from those who are going to die young and give to those who are going to die old, the transfer tends to be going from the less advantaged to the more advantaged. Unless those who live to die older are specially afflicted with very serious problems, any of us would prefer to be a person with low income who lives to age 80 rather than a rich person who dies at age 20. (A complication here is that if prosperity is increasing over time, and longevity is rising, those now elderly may be heading to less fulfilling lives on average than those young now are heading toward.) At least, from an egalitarian welfarist perspective, we should always be looking beyond the resources that people get to what effect those resources will have on their quality of life, reasonably assessed over their entire lives.

Notice also, we might see a lack of money in another way, as a good but imperfect proxy for having inadequate real freedom to live as one chooses—freedom, not welfare, being the right moral standard for assessing people's condition. On this view, having money is a partial constituent of the freedom that is what ultimately matters, and lacking money is also an indicator of probable overall freedom deficit. The relational egalitarian and welfarist egalitarian disagree on this issue, as Chapter 3 observes.

Social Programs That Encourage People to Have a Steady Labor Force Attachment

A person has greater labor force attachment, the more she is full-time employed, and when unemployed (whether as a transition to better employment or as an affliction that just falls on her), the more assiduously she seeks to find another job or engage in training with a view to securing employment.

Why should it be a goal of social policy to foster labor force attachment in its citizens? People are different. For some, paid labor or self-employment is obnoxious, and for many, the jobs we can secure are onerous even if we might fancy jobs with better features that are out of our reach. One might suppose that where people's tastes and aptitudes differ, a blanket policy of encouraging employment unfairly helps some and hurts others. One alternative policy would provide all adults with an unconditional basic income (UBI), funded by taxes on those who choose to engage in paying economic activity, and set at the highest long-term sustainable level. As its backers say, UBI aims to provide real freedom for all.

I interpret the Nordic penchant for nudging citizens toward steady employment in whatever economic niche they can find as reflecting a quietly paternalistic judgment: For most of us, taking and holding regular employment (or comparable self-employment) is on the whole good for us, whether we think so or not. For those of us who are not intrepid self-starters, work gets us going and provides structure to our lives. The alternation of work and leisure enhances the experience of leisure as a change of pace. Work often provides camaraderie and shared experience that ripen into friendship. If we work at home, we have the benefit of flexibility in organizing how and when we work. Living in a culture that is admiring of productivity, when we're productive, we get props for our self-esteem. Although bad bossing is a curse of work that we ought to seek to minimize, cooperating in team production is an achievement that in itself contributes to our good. Some of the benefits of work just noted may not be apparent to those outside the labor force. Also, among the productively engaged, recognizing the benefits of steady paid work may be downplayed, because these benefits arise from our ordinariness, our cookie-cutter humanity we all share, not from our interesting, unique individuality or our (as we usually suppose) amazing talents or virtues.

Interpreting a government tilt toward employment as reflecting judgments about what is objectively good in itself for people might be resisted. One might interpret a proemployment tilt as working to achieve high and fair levels of overall subjective preference satisfaction. But if the preferences that should count in this calculation are the preferences each individual would have for her life if she were thinking clearly and reflectively with full information, the theoretical difference between the interpretations may not make much practical difference when it comes to public policy choice. If instead the proper aim is taken to be satisfaction of whatever preferences people happen to have, that aim would be a poor fit with Nordic social democratic institutions.

There is also a moral side to the rationale for encouraging engagement in the productive economy. Benefiting from the wide productive cooperation of others, we arguably have a vague and loose but important duty to reciprocate by labor force attachment or equivalent contribution (including childrearing and caring for the infirm and volunteering for good causes). Given the immense variability of human circumstances, enforcement of it can easily become wrongly moralistic, but social norms and some state policies nudging rather than pushing people toward labor force attachment arguably are morally reasonable. In the Nordic case, it should also be mentioned that high levels of employment facilitate generous welfare state policies.

In the Nordic countries, able-bodied nonelderly adults are expected to be steadily full-time employed. This social norm is aligned with rules that limit access to social benefits to those who are employed or actively seeking work or unable to work. In recent years, the duration of unemployment benefits has been shortened. Besides income support linked to the recipient's income when employed, unemployment compensation includes active labor market policies designed to help people who lose their jobs find new employment that makes use of their existing skills and offers attractive pay and other benefits or alternatively to help these individuals retrain to develop new skills that mesh with local labor market opportunities or in other ways to match those seeking work to available jobs. Many countries provide such employment assistance, but what distinguishes the Nordic social democracies here is the amount of funding provided to them, along with their extent and (arguably) high quality. Since participation in retraining programs or in active labor market programs assisting job-seeking (for those not recovering from sickness or injury) tends to be required for eligibility for unemployment assistance, one's incentive to sustain steady labor force attachment is increased.

Programs That Foster Equality Between Men and Women by Boosting Women's Labor Force Participation and Easing the Strain of Childrearing While Employed

The Nordic country governments make available affordable early childhood pre-school education and day care for school-age children with a view to making it easier for parents of young children to combine childrearing and paid employment. This can take the form of public provision or subsidies that cap the percentage of their income that parents must pay for private provision. Along the same line, these governments mandate or subsidize paid leave for parents of newborns for their first year of life, with some percentage of the leave available only to male parents (in two-parent heterosexual families). These policies reflect research that suggests that high-quality early childhood education made available to children of lower-income parents has lasting effects on recipient children that are uncontroversially beneficial to them (Heckman 2006), research that suggests that having a full-time stay-at-home parent for the first year of one's life is important for child development (Waldfogel 2006, ch. 2), and research that suggests that for fathers, the experience of being a stay at home parent during the first year of parenthood increases their subsequent involvement in childrearing and in this way arguably eases the strain of combining paid work and parenting for their female partners (in heterosexual partnerships) (Huerta et al. 2014, Petts and Knoester 2018). Since 1998, Norway has provided a cash allowance to parents raising young children.

With the exception of Norway, which provides income support for a single parent raising children without holding or seeking employment, the Scandinavian countries have welfare policies that encourage a single parent raising children to sustain paid employment. The challenge here is to encourage egalitarian sharing within families while also being fair to single individuals and avoiding policies that have the side effect of discouraging family formation.

It is not an undue stretch to interpret the policies that encourage women's increased employment as reflecting a feminist agenda that seeks equality of status, life prospects, and opportunities across men and women. Nancy Fraser has characterized the ideal: "The key to equity in post-industrial welfare states is to make women's current life-pattern the norm for everyone. Women today often combine breadwinning and caregiving, albeit with great difficulties and strain. A post-industrial welfare state must ensure that men do the same, while redesigning institutions so as to eliminate the difficulty and strain. We might call this vision "Universal Caregiver" (Fraser 1994, 611, see also Esping-Andersen 2009). Among adult members of households, the ideal would include equal sharing of childrearing and eldercare, housework, and work that generates income, or perhaps, better, a statistically equal split of these contributions across all households, men and women on average doing equal sharing.

Universal Provision Versus Targeted Benefits

The Nordic countries are strongly linked to favoring programs that shower benefits on all citizens rather than target the poor. This feature especially marks their welfare state policies at their inception. In this spirit, health care benefits, subsidized child care, and public schools are provided on an age-related basis to all, and unemployment benefits are available to all unemployed citizens. Old age provision is universalistic only in guaranteeing a basic retirement income for all elderly, but beyond that, your pension is greater, the greater your lifetime earnings and mandated saving of part of your earnings.

Commentators often praise universal provision on the grounds that it encourages voter support for welfare state programs over the long run (compare Kenworthy 2011, 53–62; Jensen 2021). One thought is that when benefits are strongly means-tested, taxpayers will come to see themselves as the productive ones who are being forced by the state to provide charitable aid to the needy (for a different line of thought, see Moene and Wallerstein 2001). For any given level of voter willingness to fund benefits, of course, targeting that aims at the poor and specially disadvantaged will provide greater benefits for the targeted groups (Akerlof 1978). One might read proponents of universal provision as holding that it has a desirable manipulative effect on taxpayers, lulling them into a willingness to accept higher taxes that provide substantial aid to the poor than they would accept if the proposal were more straightforwardly advertised as, "You pay and the needy will benefit." Along the same line, we might also worry that stigma will attach to targeted benefits that only poor and needy people get, reducing the improvement in people's lives that the benefit brings. We should strive to avoid invidious stigma, a culture in which people disparage the down and out, even if they extend them a helping hand. Successful targeting, identifying those in dire need, inevitably divides citizens into needy and nonneedy. Making this division salient might, but does not necessarily, tend to induce the nonneedy to view themselves as superior and more worthy. As its advocates hold, universal provision may foster feelings of affinity and solidarity across citizens, a tendency for taxpayers to perceive aid recipients as "like us, just unlucky" (Rothstein 1998).

Whether means-tested programs to aid the poor will tend in practice to become mean-spirited and stingy involves an array of empirical questions, to which answers may vary with circumstances in complex ways. Another possible benefit of universal provision is savings on administrative cost—means-tested programs require bureaucratic procedures to separate those who lack means and are truly needy from others (Lindert 2021).

In recent decades, Denmark has moved increasingly to targeting redistributive social spending. Finland, Sweden, and Denmark have introduced earned income tax credit (EITC) policies, which offer tax credits to low-income people conditional on their employment. So there's at least some reason to doubt the strength, or at least the generality, of the claim about the psychological dispositions of the taxpayers that would render universalism the right strategy if and when the claim is true. There is also room for doubt as to whether there is anything morally praiseworthy in itself about universalism. Why should you prefer to get a payback for yourself from pro-poor policies you support, if you turn out not to be poor yourself?

Centralized Wage Bargaining

In the Nordic countries, wage negotiations are centralized. They "normally take place between unions representing the employees and the employer associations representing the businesses" (Jensen 2021, also Jensen and Van Kersbergen 2017). Bargains struck for an industry apply also to nonunionized workers in that sector. Compared to what happens when bargaining is done within each individual firm, or between a firm and each of its individual employees, wage differences tend to be compressed. Centralized negotiation may also foster more cooperative, less adversarial relations between unions and business firms.

Actual wage bargaining practices are more complex than just indicated. Often there is a two-tier process, with sectoral determination of baseline wages for specified types of labor, followed by firm-level negotiations making some adjustment (Bhuller et al. 2022). But the broad contrast between countries with centralized and noncentralized wage bargaining holds.

Moderate Labor Market and Product Regulation

"Moderate" needs clarification. Taxation of (1) negative externalities—harms imposed on people that prevent market exchange from reaching efficient outcomes—and of (2) rents—benefits individuals gain from filling an economic role that are unnecessary to induce them to fill that role—are forms of regulation, but high rates of taxation of these sorts shouldn't automatically qualify as immoderate. Regulation can also sometimes substitute for boosting the bargaining power of people who have too little, or approximate the outcomes people would have chosen had they been fully informed of relevant facts (or in some cases, if they had sensibly assessed relevant facts). Government regulation of business activity can steer enterprises from harmful activities such as emitting polluting factory smoke into the atmosphere, dumping toxic wastewater in rivers, subjecting employees to unsafe working conditions.

Regulation can also impose costs on business firms without bringing about any benefits. Regulation can also linger on the books when the reasons for imposing it have disappeared. The Nordic countries are noteworthy for efforts to avoid nonbeneficial regulation. Countries vary widely in how hard they make it to start up a business, how complex are the procedures involved in paying corporate taxes, how easy or hard it is to shrink their workforce or shift to a different line of product in response to market conditions, and so on. The World Bank compiles an Ease of Doing Business Index, on the basis of a survey of relevant experts, rating 189 countries on the difficulty of conducting 11 core business activities. In 2014, three of the four Nordic nations are ranked among the top ten countries, and Sweden ranked eleventh. Two other related measures, the Global Competitiveness Report and the global Innovation Index, show similar results (Kenworthy 2020, 42).

The Efficacy of Nordic Social Democratic Practices

Just having laws on the books and public policies in place that aim at improving the prospects of less advantaged members of society is not so impressive if the laws and public policies do not actually improve the life prospects of this target population. Moreover, to assess policy efficacy, besides getting an idea of the degree to which the policies achieve their intended goals, we would also like to know whether those achievements come at the expense of other values we ought to care about, and if so, what these trade-offs are.

3
Egalitarian Principles

If we are wondering whether or not the institutions and policies of Nordic social democracy are morally justified, the relevant question is, how do they stand up to correct moral principles (insofar as we can get a handle on what they are). In present and likely future circumstances, broadly speaking, are these institutions and practices the ones we should put in place, or sustain where they already exist, according to our best current understanding of what morality requires of us?

The discussion that follows is guided by a further contestable hunch. This is that sympathetic interpretation of the socialist values that emerged into view in the mid-nineteenth-century critique of capitalism yields a reliable moral compass for our time. The nineteenth-century discussions did not get it right, but they enable us to get it much closer to right. If socialist principles support Nordic social democracy over the alternatives, then morality rightly understood supports it.

Justifying this claim about socialist values would require a wide-ranging inquiry I do not even begin to undertake. There is after all no reason to suspect that a few Europeans circa 1850 had access to a special window affording them a clear view of moral truth, better than any other thinkers in other places and times had and have. I simply affirm candidate principles in a way that highlights their intuitive abstract appeal and gestures at what they imply, given the empirical facts we face and will face. You can just as well call these plausible views "egalitarian principles" if you like. This discussion employs both labels. Readers will have to make up their own minds as to how plausible they find these principles, in light of their abstract

Debating Capitalism. Richard J. Arneson and Jason Brennan, Oxford University Press.
 DOI: 10.1093/9780190076467.003.0006

plausibility and the intuitive acceptability of their implications for choice of action and public policy.

The thought here is that the rise of industrial capitalism in England and Europe in the nineteenth century, with its accompanying great increase in wealth, spurred some thinkers to discern that society need not inexorably divide into (1) a small elite living high on the hog and lording over (2) a huge mass of humanity far worse off and barely staying alive. There can be a more equal world, and a world in which almost all of us have good life prospects. Theorists and writers who were poles apart in many ways, including the radical Karl Marx and the utilitarian John Stuart Mill, shared this much.

Karl Marx

Karl Marx is famous for denouncing capitalism and proposing its abolition. One objection was that under capitalism, some individuals own productive resources such as factories and hire workers, who own no productive resources apart from their own minds and bodies. Workers laboring for capitalists produce products and services that are sold at a profit, and the employer earns a living by taking a share of this profit. This is inherently unfair and wrong—exploitive, thought Marx. The Earth and the productive resources we inherit from past generations belong to all of us together, not solely to capitalist owners of this wealth. Good luck, for which no one can properly take credit, makes some people capitalists, and similar bad luck beyond their power to control turns some people into workers. This split is unfair and irrational, and abolishing private property and organizing the economy on "communist" lines will bring about unequivocal progress, ending exploitation.

There are several ideas floating around here; let's pick out one strand. Even if sheer morally arbitrary luck makes some people capitalists and some exploited workers under present arrangements, must this be so? We could imagine wealth initially divided equally (or in any other way you regard as intrinsically fair). From there, morally innocent trade could lead to some hiring others to work on resources the hiring persons own (Roemer 1985). Take a very simple illustration. The sole productive resource is seed corn, which can be eaten for consumption and also combined with labor to grow more of the same. The economy consists of just two persons, Maria, who wants to work just enough to allow her sustainably to subsist in future, giving her ample free time each day for leisure activities she values, and Sally, who desires less free time and increased seed corn from year to year, affording her extra corn consumption she values. Starting out with equal seed corn for both Maria and Sally, more than enough for subsistence, Sally will use more seed corn than Maria and will want to work up even more, and Maria has spare seed corn that will be wasted unless someone works it up. Both benefit if Maria hires Sally to work on her extra seed corn, with both sharing some of the produce. Each person's preferences seem reasonable; as we might say, they just have different tastes.

It is hard to discern anything that should be classified as (unfair) exploitation here. The sheer fact that one person owns productive resources and makes a profit from hiring another person here does not appear to be intrinsically bad or wrong. The issue is whether you legitimately own the productive resources you say you own, and whether you are being fair in the deals and trades you make with others and not squeezing them unduly when they are squeezed by sheer bad luck—especially bad luck beyond their power to control by reasonable choices they could make. There may be other problems with capitalism, but the unfairness to which Marx (along with others) calls attention could be eliminated without the abolition of capitalism.

The contemporary Marxist philosopher Nicholas Vrousalis (2023) appeals to an example he calls the Pit. Someone has fallen into a deep pit and will drown there unless help is forthcoming. You happen on the scene and offer to rescue the drowning person if she agrees to give you a huge sum every year for the rest of her life. That's unfair, exploitative, says Vrousalis. You should just rescue the person, do the right thing. Concerning this particular example, we might well agree. But what if you have to undergo great trouble and risk to complete the rescue? Is profiting from others' bad luck always bad and wrong? Not plausibly. Think of medical personnel earning their living by treating disease. You can have power over someone, yet refrain from using it to gouge this person, and instead charge a fair price. Let's assume, in an ongoing real-world market economy, some will have asymmetric power over others. Is this a problem? From the standpoint of distributive fairness, this depends on the resulting outcomes—who ends up getting what.

In "Notes on the Gotha Program," Marx states that in a higher phase of communism, society can write on its banner, "From each according to his ability, to each according to his needs" (Marx 1977, 565–570). This says, in the egalitarian society, each contributes equally in proportion to her ability, and receives back benefits that accord each equal fulfillment of her needs. This norm goes beyond equal opportunity, requiring equal outcomes measured by ability and need. (A reciprocity condition also appears to be implicit in the norm. Equal contribution, assessed in terms of conscientious effort, merits equal fulfillment.)

Pondering this principle, Jon Elster considers and rejects the possibility that Marx is describing a social world beyond justice, in which people doing just as they like bring it about that everyone's needs are fully satisfied. Elster's surmise is that "it is not only more charitable but also more plausible to interpret the needs principle as a statement of welfare egalitarianism" (Elster 1986, 100). The thought is that Marx is clearly an egalitarian of some sort. And the Gotha Program critique banner slogan, as Elster reads it, indicates that the distribution of resources across persons ought to be in the service of fair distribution of the welfare of persons that resource distribution enables. Elster observes that income and other resources only matter to the extent that they provide us with welfare. He adds that according to Marx, individual welfare—what in itself makes a person's life go better for her rather than worse—should be understood as self-realization. An individual realizes herself insofar as she freely develops and exercises her valuable capacities (Elster 1986, 43–46).

But go back to Vrousalis and the Pit example. He reads Marx very differently from how Elster interprets him. Suppose we could set up social life as a bunch of pits, and everywhere some have arbitrary power over others, to help those at the bottom of some pit escape this plight or not, as the power-holders decide. In any realistic scenario, the outcomes of this arrangement will be systematically bad for those over whom others wield such power, but even if we imagine that somehow the distributive outcomes are nice, according to Vrousalis there would still be a huge objection to the distributively ideal pit society: It's bad and wrong for social arrangements to put some under the thumb of others in this way. We should be relating as equals, with none having unchecked, arbitrary power over the lives of others. Vrousalis's Marx holds that capitalism systematically and unavoidably sustains hierarchies of unequal power that we could otherwise avoid, and that is justification for its abolition.

Whether or not this opinion is correct, and regardless of whether Elster's Marx or Vrousalis's Marx better captures Marx's thinking all things considered, two different conceptions of egalitarianism can be discerned here: (1) the welfarist egalitarian ideal of a community of individuals all together flourishing and (2) the relational egalitarian ideal of a community of free and equal citizens. As the *Communist Manifesto* puts it, a community in which "the free development of each shall be the condition of the free development of all" (Marx 1977, 219–247). Notice that this phrasing is ambiguous—it might be affirming (1) or (2).

John Stuart Mill

Any attempt to recruit John Stuart Mill to the broad socialist cause might seem an unprofitable effort at uphill sledding. He's a stalwart defender of a market economy with private ownership of productive resources. But that is not dispositive. Mill's vision of a desirable economic future envisages capitalism without capitalists—a gradual transition driven by the market choices of many individual workers toward an economy entirely or mainly consisting of worker-owned and worker-controlled cooperative enterprises (Mill 1848, Dahl 1985).

More important for interpreting where Mill stood is his uncertain embrace of egalitarianism. At the level of fundamental moral principle, Mill never retracts his commitment to utilitarianism. In a canonical statement of this position, he asserts that "actions are right in proportion as they tend to promote happiness; wrong as they tend to produce the reverse of happiness" (*Utilitarianism*, ch. 2). The happiness that bears on choice is not that of the agent only, but of all who might be affected by her choice. We should evaluate actions, institutions, social practices, and public policies by the same standard. The ultimate standard is maximization of the sum total of happiness or good quality of life (welfare, well-being) attained by persons. On this view, common-sense moral rules give an agent reason for choice of action only insofar as complying with the rule, such as telling the truth or keeping one's promise, would bring about better results (more total happiness) than anything else the agent might instead have done.

But Mill never squarely faces the issue of whether what is in itself morally right, what an agent always has most moral reason to do, is to maximize *the total of happiness summed across persons.* In chapter 5 of *Utilitarianism*, which purports to address the objection that maximizing the total sum of human happiness conflicts with justice or fairness, Mill never discusses the worry that maximizing the total might conflict with fair distribution of happiness across individual persons (Mill 1861). Nor does this issue get treated in Mill's works applying utilitarianism to social problems and public policy matters. In *The Subjection of Women*, arguing for the complete equality of legal rights for women and men, Mill nowhere suggests that if legal inequality worked to maximize the general welfare, we should go with inequality (Mill 1869). Mill's views on policy seem to presuppose a tilt toward equality as right in itself that he never explicitly affirms.

Could a more equal distribution with a lower total be morally superior to a higher total less evenly distributed? Mill does not tell us. Nor does Mill consider other fair distribution issues, such as whether a world in which the morally undeserving fare better and the morally deserving fare worse would be morally better or worse in itself to some degree than an otherwise similar world in which the morally deserving saints fare better and the morally undeserving sinners fare worse. (To be fair, in *Utilitarianism*, Mill raises a related issue, namely, whether virtue is more worthy of promotion than happiness (Mill 1861, ch. 2). He replies that character traits are instrumentally not intrinsically valuable, and that the traits we should prize as virtues are those that are happiness-increasing, not those that are happiness-diminishing. He could take the same line on making distribution more equal that he seems to take on rewarding the morally virtuous. This stance should not budge anyone who starts with pro-equality or pro-deservingness leanings.)

So Mill plumps for straight utilitarianism but advances no arguments against modifying utilitarianism by affirming that we ought to be promoting fair distribution of welfare and identifying fair distribution with equal distribution. Moving onto that path, we would be embracing welfarist egalitarianism (WE), which holds that we ought at the fundamental level to be valuing both more welfare and more equal distribution of it and maximizing some intuitively plausible balancing of these two values. In a slogan, morality all things considered requires maximizing equality-weighted individual well-being summed across persons.

Mill, a great liberal theorist, prominently champions individual liberty, but in chapter 1 of *On Liberty* (1859), he states emphatically, "I regard utility as the ultimate appeal on all ethical questions, but it must be utility in the largest sense, grounded in the permanent interests of man as a progressive being." This leaves open what is utility (individual welfare/well-being) "in the largest sense." Utility in a too small sense would seem to be welfare hedonically construed—pleasure net of pain. That's inadequate, and he elsewhere (1861, ch. 2) seeks to repair the inadequacy by distinguishing quality and quantity of pleasure. Pleasures can be greater or smaller in quantity, and also differ in quality according to the character of their source. Pleasures brought about by development and exercise of the more valuable capacities of persons are higher in quality, and quality and quantity of pleasure/enjoyment both affect the noninstrumental value of an episode of pleasure—the degree to which it in itself makes a person's life go better for her. In *On Liberty*, higher quality pleasure is identified with the pleasures of freely developing one's valuable individual capabilities.

This is ingenious, but in brief, it seems to be both too narrowly hedonistic and insufficiently hedonistic. Too narrowly hedonistic: Mill's considered view is that nothing in itself makes a person's life go better for her unless it includes experience of pleasure. But achievements, love, and friendship are worth having in one's life, in themselves make it better, even if entirely unaccompanied by pleasure.

Mill's view is also insufficiently hedonistic. His qualitative hedonism fails to register the fact that the experience of simple low-quality pleasure/enjoyment in itself increases one's welfare/well-being and indeed significantly boosts how well one's life is going for one. Consider eating a greasy cheeseburger with pleasure, or drinking coffee with a rush of enjoyment, or experiencing a simple sexual orgasm. Pleasure is not the only intrinsically good thing in life, but it is one significantly good thing.

These simple modifications of Mill's view transform it into what is called an objective list conception of individual welfare/well-being (Fletcher 2016). On this view, there are things that are in themselves prudentially good and bad for you, and the more your life overall contains the good things and avoids the bad things, the better overall your life goes for you. Mill and Marx both affirm an objective conception of welfare (you can be mistaken about what is in itself good for you); both seem to take a too narrow view of what objective goods there are.

Besides wavering from his proclaimed utilitarianism toward endorsing fair distribution of well-being, Mill's writing also shows signs of deviating from WE altogether by commitment to equal rights including rights to liberty and equality of opportunity between men and women. Like Marx, Mill may be undecided between welfarist and relational versions of egalitarianism.

Welfarist and Relational Egalitarianisms

Why egalitarianism? In broad terms, the idea is that all beings with rational agency capacities (cognitive, volitional, affective, and moral) at or above a threshold level and within a range qualify as persons who should regard and treat each other as fundamental equals (Rawls 1999a, 441–445, Arneson 2024). Most normal humans are persons throughout most of their lives. A qualification is that human children, though undeniably persons, are only potentially fundamental equals while developing into adults. An aspect of equality is that it is equally morally important that each person's life goes well. Beyond this common foundation, there are two rival conceptions of what regarding and treating one another as equals requires: welfarist and relational.

According to WE, what each is owed is equal consideration and concern, which requires trying to bring it about that each person's life goes better for her rather than worse, and to some degree, equally as well as the lives of others. The measure of going well is in terms of what one seeks insofar as one is striving to be prudent, namely, individual welfare or well-being. High well-being is good quality of life. There are different views as to what in itself boosts well-being. Some hold that it is getting what you want for its own sake, satisfying your noninstrumental desires over the course of your life. But it seems our lives can go badly by wanting and attaining the wrong things. This thought suggests an objective list conception of one's good: There are some things, such as friendship and love, valuable achievements of various kinds, knowledge, and enjoyment, and the more of these things you get over the course of your life, the better your life goes for you—the higher your lifetime well-being. The discussions of Marx and Mill in this section push toward the same view.

The simplest WE says that what one always has most reason to do is what would maximize a balance of the goals of greater well-being for people and more equal distribution of well-being across people. This makes WE a close cousin of utilitarianism. Whereas utilitarianism says one always morally ought to do what would maximize the total welfare of persons, WE says one ought to maximize the equality-weighted well-being total (giving weight to compressing the distribution of well-being across persons). But there is a large family of views clustered around this one. These members of the WE family all hold that morality includes a significant impartial beneficence principle, telling each of us to improve the world by boosting equality-weighted well-being, but adding some familiar constraints and options. Constraints are rules saying it is not permissible, up to some point, to act beneficently when doing so would wrongfully harm some persons in certain ways. Options are moral rules that say it is permissible not to act beneficently, to some degree, but instead to favor oneself or be partial toward those to whom one has special ties.

In contrast to WE, relational egalitarianism (RE) holds that regarding and treating one another as fundamental equals are constituted by relating as equals—building and sustaining equal social relationships. Elizabeth Anderson (1999) holds that equality is best interpreted as democratic equality—continuously enabling all members of society to participate fully on equal terms in a genuinely democratic social order. Samuel Scheffler writes that equality is opposed "to oppression, to heritable hierarchies of social status, to ideas of caste, to class privilege and the rigid stratification of classes, and to the undemocratic distribution of power" (Scheffler 2003, 22). He adds that "as a social ideal," relational equality "holds that a human society must be conceived as a cooperative arrangement among equals, each of whom enjoys the same social standing." Niko Kolodny stipulates that hierarchy "consists of asymmetries of power and authority, as well as disparities of regard" (2023, 1). Kolodny holds that hierarchy is bad and wrong unless "tempered" by various factors such as being costless to exit or being regulated by a political order in which all citizens have equal opportunity to influence.

There are many versions of RE (and of views in the neighborhood) on offer. Without making any claim to full coverage of these varieties, the discussion here anchors to the idea that we relate as equals to the degree that we sustain a society in which all are equally and substantially free to live as they choose, each living according to her own conception of what is worth seeking in life, and in which matters of public concern that should be decided for all are decided by all on equal terms, by genuinely democratic decision-making, which involves all citizens having equal opportunity for political influence (EOPI).

One articulated version of these ideas appears in the doctrine advanced by the preeminent liberal egalitarian philosopher of the twentieth century, John Rawls. Rawls makes no compromises with utilitarian thinking, so his view presents a strong contrast with the approach of WE. He writes, "Each person possesses an inviolability founded on justice that even the welfare of society as a whole cannot override. For this reason justice denies that the loss of freedom for some is made right by a greater good shared by others" (Rawls 1999a, 3). This correctly states Rawls's position, but that position also denies that a loss of basic freedom for some is made right by a greater good enjoyed by those same people. Freedom trumps, or better, freedom rightly interpreted and specified in his two principles trumps all other values.

Rawls affirms that a just set of social arrangements must satisfy three principles nested in strict order of priority. First, society sustains certain basic liberties for all including freedom of speech and thought, freedom of association, the rule of law, and the right to a democratic say and to EOPI. EOPI, or fair value of political liberty as Rawls calls it, is satisfied when, roughly speaking, all equally politically talented and politically ambitious citizens have the same chances of success at being politically influential. This strong equal opportunity principle requires that all normal adults have an equally weighted vote and equal access to informal resources for influencing others including money and free time (or same chances of gaining these). This might be done by equalizing people's holdings of money and free time or by preventing these resource inequalities from generating unequal opportunity to influence political decision-making. As a second priority, Rawls affirms Fair Equality of Opportunity (FEO), which obtains among members of society when "those who have the same level of talent and ability and the same willingness to use these gifts should have the same prospects of success regardless of their social class of origin" (2001, 44). Rawls adds that "In all parts of society there are to be roughly the same prospects of culture and achievement for all those similarly motivated and endowed." FEO is strong medicine, a radical principle of substantive equal opportunity, and arguably what Martin Luther King Jr. meant to affirm when he called for equality of opportunity for all in his famous "I have a Dream" speech. All those with equal native talent potential and equal ambition must have the same chances of attaining positions that confer unequal shares of social and economic resources. As a third priority, Rawls further affirms that all positions that confer these unequal advantages must work effectively to make the social and economic resource holdings of the worst off in this respect as large as possible.

Rawls's views contrast starkly with WE. Flourishing in the sense of living a life that is good for one, high in well-being, does not register at all as a social justice value. It is conceivable, if unlikely, that in a perfectly just Rawlsian society, all are secure in moral rights to liberties, a genuinely democratic say, strong equal opportunity, and fair shares of general-purpose resources, but none attains any well-being. Each is free to pursue her idea of the good life with Rawlsian-fair resources, not necessarily to have any success in the pursuit.

WE flips this priority entirely around. Moral rights and duties, constraints not to harm and options to pursue one's life plan and refrain from advancing the good of others, democratic liberties, and so on, are valued highly, but as instrumentally not intrinsically morally valuable—as means to bringing about increasing good lives for people with good fairly distributed across them. Many compromises between WE and RE are possible, but their principled opposition is profoundly strong.

We should notice that commitment to freedom of speech along with basic civil liberties transcends the WE versus RE conflict. An important reason to uphold free speech along with basic civil liberties is that, whether or not it facilitates fulfillment of whatever moral values and principles we currently embrace, a regime of free speech and closely allied freedoms is needed to help us over time identify better moral values and principles than anyone currently recognizes, if such there be.

It may appear that facilitating life aim fulfillment rather than the narrower idea of individual well-being is the better social justice aim. Why shouldn't we be enabling individuals to attain whatever they care about (so long as they aren't thereby violating others' rights)? One concern surfaces when one looks at the implications of life aim fulfillment when some seek only their narrow self-interest and others seek broader goals such as the common good, equal fulfillment of the moral rights of all, or distributive fairness. Seeking to equalize fulfillment of some people's selfish goals and other people's unselfish goals evenhandedly is itself unfair. Another concern is that some people's life aims, whether self-interested or altruistic, make no sense, or are just silly or (we judge) not worth pursuing. Rawls himself uses the example of a person whose fundamental life aim is to count the blades of grass on courthouse lawns, endlessly.

Rawls's freedom-centered liberal egalitarianism also contrasts sharply with right-wing freedom-centered—or better, property-centered—views (Nozick 1974, Brennan 2012). This family of views understands legitimate, morally valuable freedom as closely tied to strong rights of private ownership that are associated with an uncompromising affirmation of a capitalist market economy. On this view, the core tenet is that each adult person has a moral right to choose and act as she wishes with whatever she legitimately owns, so long as she does not thereby violate certain moral rights of others. These constraining rights are given by a list; each person has moral rights not to suffer theft of her property, fraud in transactions, breach of contract, unconsented to physical damage to her person or property, trespass—or coercive threats of any of the preceding. Each person fully owns her own body and is under no enforceable obligation to use it for the benefit of others. Each person can acquire full bequeathable ownership of material stuff by appropriation of unowned stuff and by voluntary transfer from others. Each person may forfeit some or all of her rights by violations of the rights of others and may transfer any and all of her rights to others or waive any or all of her rights.

Egalitarianism, of either the relational or welfarist variety, opposes property-oriented rights doctrines. Notice that the outcome of a series of voluntary market exchanges and transactions among property owners could turn out to be almost anything. Sally might end up owning all the marbles, and everybody else with none. Or more realistically, wealth might give some increasing advantages and ever greater wealth, over time, while some fall increasingly far behind. In contrast, Rawls holds that each of us is bound to cooperate with others to sustain basic institutions that protect and promote basic freedoms including EOPI, strong equality of opportunity, and making the least advantaged as well off as possible. Rawls suggests that these arrangements are what we would choose if fairly situated behind a veil of ignorance that blocks us from knowing whether we happen to be specially well placed with special advantages or poorly placed and disadvantaged.

The welfarist egalitarian will insist that we are legitimately morally bound by enforceable obligations to help others in peril, for example, the child who slips and falls in your swimming pool when you alone are in position rescue him from drowning. "Self-ownership" gives way here: The child has a right that you move your body in certain ways to save him. Security in one's property and in contracts freely made are welfare-enhancing and justified on that basis, except when overriding property rights is needed to advance the general welfare understood to include fair distribution of it across individuals.

The Bogy of Equality: WE Clarified

Scratching the verbal surface of many social justice ideals advanced as warranting coercive intervention, one finds a preference for equality of outcome as such: Everyone should have the same according to some appropriate standard. But what is morally valuable about everyone having the same? Some find it obvious that this is a rhetorical question and the correct answer to it is a resounding "Nothing at all!". Granted, in particular circumstances, equality might have instrumental value. If there are five people, each one will die unless she receives one full dose of a lifesaving medicine, and five doses of the medicine are on hand, equally distributing one dose to each of the five results in the nice outcome in which all survive. But supposing we had only four doses of the lifesaving medicine, distributing what we have equally to all five results in none getting a full dose and none surviving. The example might prompt the thought, equal distribution in itself not only lacks great moral value, but it lacks any value at all.

Addressing the specific ideal of equal income, Harry Frankfurt suggests a broader claim, to the effect that it does not in itself matter morally, how one person's monetary condition compares to that of others, and a fortiori, it does not in itself matter morally, whether one person's monetary condition is equal to that of others (Frankfurt 2015, 1–62). Frankfurt further holds that what any individual rationally ought to care about is *not* how her condition compares with that of others. What it does make sense to care about is whether one has enough resources for one's purposes, as indicated by the point at which, given how much one has and one's plans for these resources, one reasonably, given the ensemble of one's ends, declines actively to seek to gain more.

Nor according to Frankfurt is there, beyond individuals' subjective concerns, an impersonal moral imperative to achieve equality. If inequality were morally bad or wrong in itself, it would be bad no matter how well off everyone was. If we were all at least super-rich, but some among us were super-super-rich, the gap between those with more and those with less would be a moral affront, just as the same gap would be between the resource shares of those in extreme poverty and those comfortably well off. But surely the inequality among the enormously well off is of no concern at all from the moral standpoint, so it cannot be the gap between those better off and those worse off that morally matters. Instead we should see that in the second case, the sensible ground for moral concern is that some are horribly short of having enough. So urges Frankfurt.

If equality in people's condition were in itself morally valuable, then when we are comparing people's condition along some important dimension of value, it might be that moving closer to equality along that value dimension is sufficiently valuable for its own sake to warrant coercive enforcement. Coercing people into an equal condition might be a worthy goal, even if it brings about no further improvement in other ways. But if equality is in itself strictly a "Don't care" from the moral standpoint, advancing equality for its own sake never warrants any coercive enforcement. This issue matters if we are trying to figure out what our stance should be toward the outcomes of capitalist market exchange.

The puzzle about whether equality in people's condition is in itself morally valuable arises no matter by what standard we are measuring people's condition. Frankfurt uses the example of equality in how much money individuals have, but as long as we have a unitary scale for measuring how badly off people are along some dimension, the issue arises. Egalitarians of individual welfare and egalitarians regarding individual freedom might be troubled by Frankfurt's doubt. Moreover, if each person has the same moral rights, several of them, varying in importance, one might hold that it is always a good thing if more people's rights are fulfilled to a greater rather than a lesser extent, but deny that everyone's having the same degree of rights fulfillment is in itself valuable.

Another way of stating the Frankfurt worry: Commitment to the claim that equality of condition across people by some measure is morally desirable in itself commits one to the idea that making those who are now better off worse off, without securing any gain for those now worse off, improves the overall situation in at least one significant respect, by bringing people's condition closer to equal. If we balk at this, and hold that such leveling down does not make the resulting state of affairs better in any respect, we seem to be rejecting equality in people's condition of any sort as a moral ideal.

However, these appearances are misleading, and denial of the value of equality is overblown. The somewhat roundabout discussion that follows will support this claim. This discussion will mostly focus on equality of welfare (people's individual levels of well-being), but the equality versus priority issue to be outlined applies generally. One could be prioritarian regarding the values of freedom, rights fulfillment, and so on.

The leveling down objection prompts some to turn from affirming a norm of distributive equality to a norm of distributive priority (Parfit 1991, Arneson 2022). Equality says, it is morally undesirable if some are worse off than others. Priority says, gains in welfare (well-being) for a person are more valuable, the worse off the person would otherwise be, in absolute terms. Equality is concerned with people's relative condition. Not so priority. Otherwise put, priority holds that a benefit one could gain for a person is morally more valuable, (1) the larger the benefit and (2) the worse off the person would otherwise be, in absolute terms, over the course of her life, absent this benefit. Here we can count avoiding a loss for a person as an instance of gaining a benefit. Priority will never count making someone worse off without making anyone else better off as possibly an improvement. Priority never recommends leveling down.

A morality that simply affirmed equality of condition would be crazy. Everyone's being equally miserable, or even equally dead, would be preferable to an alternative situation in which everyone is alive and very well off, but some are more well off than others.

A noncrazy or pluralist egalitarian values two things: (1) people being better off and (2) people being more equally well off. A prioritarian values (1) increase in the total extent to which people are better off. In addition, the prioritarian (2) assigns greater value to gaining a one-unit increase in the total well-being of someone's life (or avoiding a one-unit decrease), the less the total amount of well-being this person would otherwise attain over the course of her life. The question arises, is there more than a verbal disagreement here? Are the prioritarian and the pluralist egalitarian disagreeing substantively about the assessment of states of affairs, or are they really saying the same thing in different words? If the prioritarian and the egalitarian both hold that we have some duty to choose courses of action that will make the outcomes of choice better rather than worse, will they ever disagree about what courses of action to choose, in order to conform to that duty?

This question turns out to have a slightly complicated answer. The economist Marc Fleurbaey (2015) has demonstrated an interesting result. Suppose that we are choosing among actions each of which for sure would bring about one definite outcome if we choose it. Then "any prioritarian will always find some egalitarian view [that is, some pluralist view valuing more welfare as well as more equal distribution of it] which reaches the same practical conclusion about all possible cases, although possibly for different reasons." So we seem to be looking at a tempest in a teapot. To reiterate: By "all possible cases" Fleurbaey means, all cases in which it is certain, for any act we might choose, what the outcome of carrying out that act would be.

But suppose we are choosing among risky alternatives. Then the views can yield conflicting advice about what action or policy to choose. So there is still significant disagreement.

But the prioritarian and egalitarian are both broadly egalitarian, in that both affirm a significant claim, called "Pigou-Dalton" in the terminology of welfare economics (Adler and Holtug 2019). This says: A pure welfare transfer from a better off to a worse off person that does not reduce this benefit, provided the transfer does not switch their relative positions and does not affect anyone else's welfare levels, is always an improvement. Recall, the priority view identifies greater value in bringing about a benefit for a person, the worse off in absolute terms she would otherwise be. This implies that even though the prioritarian attaches no value or disvalue in itself to how one person's condition compares to that of others, by simple arithmetic, the prioritarian must judge instrumentally valuable a pure transfer of welfare from a better off to a worse off person, as asserted by Pigou-Dalton.

In light of this agreement, the simplest version of WE can be characterized as morally favoring the maximization either of equality-weighted or priority-weighted aggregate well-being summed across people.

Does this clarification do anything to undercut the anti-egalitarian position that Frankfurt eloquently champions? Why can't the anti-egalitarian widen the attack so it rejects Pigou-Dalton and priority along with the simple equality doctrine that says it is morally desirable in itself that everyone be equally well off?

In reply, you can take this line, but it is hard to swallow. Imagine that you have no choice but to impose some harm, such as contracting an infectious disease that will for sure worsen the life of whoever gets it by the same amount, on either a homeless young person whose life has been terrible up to now and unavoidably will not greatly improve or on someone who has already lived a long and great life loaded with fulfillments anyone would envy. No one else will be affected. Is it really plausible to hold that there is nothing morally worse about the state of affairs in which the much worse off person suffers this further bad thing, by comparison with the alternative state of affairs in which this bad falls instead on the already very fortunate individual, where this shift still leaves the person with the hellish quality of life still far worse off overall than the other?

Pigou-Dalton is a fairly weak premise. It allows that a transfer of welfare from a better off to a worse off individual that ever so vanishingly slightly reduces the benefit transferred, is not an improvement. Roughly speaking, I would say it makes sense to regard as truly egalitarian only versions of priority and equality that attach significant weight to bringing about gains or avoiding losses for worse offs. There is a judgment call to make here about how much weight is too much to attach and how much is too little. (Here as elsewhere in normative political theory, how much comparative importance should be attached to values that may be traded off against each other is a big deal in terms of determining the shape of one's theory, but philosophy offers slight help as to how to identify more and less accurate judgment.)

But nothing blocks the prioritarian and the egalitarian from being close comrades on this significance issue each must settle to arrive at a determinate view. And if they are close comrades on this issue, we should regard them as close comrades, period, despite their disagreement on the question of whether it matters in itself how one person's condition compares to that of another. For purposes of assessing capitalism, democracy, Nordic social democracy, and alternatives, I see the broad egalitarians, whether they affirm pluralistic equality or the priority view, as reasonably to be on the same side of the barricades. The crucial divide is between egalitarians on one side and anti-egalitarians and nonegalitarians on the other.

Another clarification is needed here. Equality and priority might be views on the issue, how to assess outcomes or possible states of the world on an impartial moral basis. Nothing would be claimed so far about what policies and actions one ought to choose and carry out. Let's stipulate that the broad egalitarian position asserts that each of us is under a strong though not necessarily overriding enforceable beneficence obligation to improve the world, bring about impartially better outcomes. The evaluation of outcomes is not then an idle wheel in determining the right choice of policy and action.

At the limit, a morality that takes this beneficence obligation seriously might affirm it as the sole moral principle—one ought always to choose an act among the available alternatives that would bring about an outcome morally no worse, by impartial moral assessment, than the outcome of anything else one might instead do. Here, this abstract maximizing norm is yoked to the egalitarian welfarist standard of outcome assessment. But I suggest that the crucial moral divide, taking this clarification on board, is between those who accept, and those who reject, a significant weighty moral beneficence requirement that understands the aim of beneficence to be improving the world by bringing about more good quality life for people, with good more fairly (equally) distributed across them.

4
Defending Nordic Social Democracy

What would it even mean to assess basic political and social arrangements in a society according to their success in bringing about the welfare egalitarian goal—more good quality life enjoyed by people with good quality life fairly distributed across people? The degree to which someone's life goes better for her, all things considered, in objective list terms, is not directly observable.

We might hope to cope with this problem by employing observable proxies for the not readily observable all things considered individual levels of well-being that we care about. Having more income enables a person to obtain more of what she believes will enhance her welfare. Having more education tends to improve a person's ability to gather information relevant to decisions as to what will advance her welfare and her ability to make better decisions on the basis of the information she has. Having a longer life, especially more years of life with good health, is having a generally excellent means to boosting one's lifetime welfare. The answers that a person gives to survey questions along the lines of "How satisfactory for you is your life as a whole?" provide information about her beliefs as to how well her life is going for her. We surmise that if people score well on many such indicators, their lives are probably going well for them.

Assessing the extent to which social and political arrangements fulfill welfare egalitarianism, we give extra weight to the impact of these arrangements on people who are heading toward lives that will be overall worse off in welfare. In this exercise, I make a further simplification. I assume that the truly disadvantaged, those whose lives will end up worse off than others without our help, will be a greater fraction of people, the lower their wealth and income. This is

Debating Capitalism. Richard J. Arneson and Jason Brennan, Oxford University Press.
 DOI: 10.1093/9780190076467.003.0007

of course a gross simplification. As is commonly said, the best things in life are free. But almost all of these best things have prerequisites that cost money and usually a lot of money. And many less than best things that contribute to welfare are pretty readily accessible by spending money.

Consider studies measuring inequality in the yearly incomes of members of society in different years. A series of such snapshot studies does not directly tell us how any individual persons are faring over time. Suppose the bottom 10% of the population have a larger share of national income in 2025 than in 2020. That finding is consistent with the persons falling into the "bottom ten percent" classification in 2020 being entirely different persons from those falling in that same classification in 2015. When considering a variety of measures of equality of one sort or another in societies, welfare egalitarians will be interested in how the measures bear on how well off an individual becomes over her life as a whole—how high is her lifetime individual well-being, and how that compares with how others are doing.

The Nordic countries stand out as achieving greater equality according to a variety of ways of measuring aspects of it. One is the Gini coefficient of disposable income (how much income one has after taxes and transfers). The Gini measures how much of the total of this income would have to be redistributed so that everyone has the same. It ranges from zero to one. A companion measure compares the ratio of the disposable income at the 90th percentile to the disposable income at the 50th percentile along with comparing the 50th percentile disposable income to the 10th percentile.

Another commonly employed inequality measure is relative poverty. The relative poverty rate in a country is the proportion of households whose disposable income is below 50% (or in some studies, 60%) of the median disposable income in that country. We can contrast this with an absolute poverty rate in a country, which is the proportion of its households whose disposable income in constant dollars is below what would be required to purchase a reference bundle of basic necessities in that country. The absolute poverty rate probably more closely tracks what most of us intuitively have in mind when we imagine people being impoverished—whether or not one's own basic needs are met does not vary depending on the degree to which other people's basic needs are met. But note that reference bundles utilized in studies differ from country to country and are also revised periodically, so in practice both absolute and relative poverty measures have a relative poverty component.

The discussion that follows tries to look at the performance of the Nordic countries from different angles. Here's the upshot: The Nordic countries of Denmark, Sweden, Norway, and Finland do more than other countries to equalize the post-tax post-transfer incomes of their citizens, reduce gaps between the opportunities of women and men, boost the employment rate of working-age citizens, and increase the educational opportunities and (arguably) mobility prospects of low-income citizens. We might doubt that equalizing conditions between better-off and worse-off citizens is in itself desirable, since you could render people more equal by worsening conditions of better offs without bringing about any gains for worse offs. But the Nordic nations boost equality while maintaining economic growth in gross domestic product (GDP). If you make the pie bigger while dividing it more equally, and if increases and decreases in the shares of "pie" that individuals get are correlated with well-being increases and decreases, you will be boosting equality-weighted well-being, which is what morality requires according to welfarist egalitarianism. And the Nordic countries do this better than other countries and have been performing well by this measure since the 1970s at least. To be sure, even if these claims are correct, they don't establish that Nordic institutions and public policies are causally responsible for bringing about this morally nice result. But if we have at least a plausible account of how Nordic institutions and policies comprising a generous welfare state ought to get credit for causing the desirable outcomes just described, mere possibilities to the effect that this credit is not deserved do not very much dent this defense of Nordic social democracy (NSD).

A more complete assessment than this chapter attempts would compare the performance of NSD to wealthy country regime types other than (1) countries like the United States, the United Kingdom, and Canada, with lower taxes and less pro-poor social spending and greater inequality and (2) the conservative Southern European welfare states that support a male breadwinner family pattern and whose high taxes and state spending are oriented in favor of insiders over outsiders and are not especially pro-poor. For example, consider East Asian nations including Japan, Korea, and Taiwan, characterized by low rates of taxation and little pro-poor public social spending accompanied by a rather egalitarian distribution of pre-tax income and hence also of post-tax post-transfer income. The contingencies that at least for now have shaped these outcomes include (1) low levels of inequality of land ownership when each of these nations began rapid economic development at some point after World War II, (2) good quality primary and secondary education for all in place as their economic growth began, (3) virtually no immigration, and (4) a comparative advantage in unskilled labor when they underwent export-led economic growth (as summarized in Lindert 2021, at 227 and generally 225–9). This adds up to historical good luck, which other nations may be unable to emulate. These East Asian countries are marked by very high life expectancy. They score low on measures of women's equality including women's labor force participation rates, the gender wage gap, and division of household and childrearing labor across cohabiting husbands and wives.

Economic Equality

A study of post-tax post-transfer income in 2005 of households at the 10th percentile of this distribution in an array of rich countries, with incomes adjusted for purchasing power parity and household size, shows Denmark and Norway at the top, with Sweden and Finland not far behind. Similar results appear in studies of relative poverty (the fraction of households with income below 60% of the median household income) (Kenworthy 2020). In rich countries having institutions that are more social democratic (closer to the Nordics), relative poverty is less. Another snapshot of living conditions among the poor in an array of rich countries is provided by a 2005 study showing the percentage of people in a country who report one or more of several significant material deprivations. Sweden, Denmark, Norway, and Finland had the smallest percentages (also Kenworthy 2020). A 2018 OECD report reports similar findings. The Gini for disposable (post-tax post-transfer) income in the United States is 33% higher than for the average of Denmark, Sweden, and Norway, and similar results obtain if you compare the ratio of disposable income at the 90th and 50th percentiles and also at the 50th and 10th percentiles in these countries (cited in Jensen 2021; see also Jensen and van Kersbergen 2017).

There appear to be two drivers of higher disposable income equality in Nordic countries. One source is greater tax and egalitarian transfer of pre-tax earnings, especially compared to the United States and the United Kingdom, and other liberal market societies (and conservative Southern European welfare states, especially Italy). Another driver is greater equality of pre-tax earnings in the Nordic countries. It's not a surprise that if you tax and transfer in the direction of equality, you get more equality. What explains the somewhat greater equality of pre-tax earnings in the Nordics?

Social scientists point to high employment rates among those whose pre-tax earnings are lower, enhanced skills in the members of this group, and the effects of centralized wage bargaining in Nordic countries. Centralized wage bargaining may have the largest impact (Mogstad et al. 2025). All of these are intended aims of government policies.

The Nordics provide pre-school high-quality child care for children and generously funded (as a percentage of GDP) public education, with equal per-pupil expenses, resulting in a high level of skill acquisition in youth entering employment. Provision of pre-school child care along with generous paid parental leave from employment following the birth of a child, and affordable subsidized availability of after-school child care for primary school children, works to boost employment, especially among women and in particular women raising children. Active labor market programs, to be described below, help those who become unemployed regain paid employment.

Centralized wage bargaining is prevalent in Europe, more so in Scandinavian countries, but not so much in English-speaking wealthy countries. Representatives of unionized employees and of employers' associations in an industry or sector of the economy meet and negotiate wage bargains that are then applied generally across most workers in the industry or sector. In a second phase of bargaining, adjustments are made at the level of the individual firm; typically, this involves sharing productivity gains in the particular firm between wages and profits. Compared to what occurs when wage bargaining takes place only at the level of the individual firm or between a single employer and her employees, centralized bargaining tends to compress wages.

These features of Nordic countries may be mutually reinforcing. High employment rates make it cheaper, and so more palatable, for taxpayers to fund generous government assistance to the unemployed. A high level of skill and ability in the workforce, including the less skilled and able fraction of the work force, makes it more palatable for employers to accept some wage compression and high wages for the less skilled. Centralized wage bargaining, establishing a floor to wages in various types of work in an industry or sector, puts pressure on less efficient firms, burdened by the wage floor, requiring them to either become more productive or go out of business (Barth et al. 2014).

Equality and Economic Growth

If equalization by tax and transfer reduces economic productivity and growth, over time, we will be equalizing a stagnant or declining national income. It's plausible to surmise that regularly and expectably taking from the rich and giving to the poor reduces the incentives of both rich and poor to be economically productive. In the long run, the incomes of all are reduced, compared to what they would have been had we refrained from this redistribution (Cowen 2018). In this scenario, equality-weighted well-being is definitely not being maximized. But the historical experience of countries that sustain generous welfare states does not show any tendency for these big-spending countries to suffer reduced economic growth as just described. What explains this?

The broad answer is that welfare states both collect taxes and spend the funds collected in ways that manage to be growth-promoting as well as pro-poor. The negative incentive effects likely exist (and might become severe if Robin Hood policies were pushed beyond some point not yet reached), but are in actual practice outweighed by offsetting tendencies. Too much inequality might also do nothing to help growth and, at some level, impede it (Lindert and Williamson 2016). In this balancing endeavor, the Nordic approach contains lessons in how to do it right (for an alternative view on inequality and growth, see Alesina and Rodrik 1994).

One piece of the puzzle is that welfare states impose high taxes, but these overall are close to proportional, not strongly progressive. Also, these states rely on income taxes and value-added tax (VAT) on consumption, including on kinds of consumption that impose costs on others (such as alcohol, gasoline, and tobacco), eschewing taxes on corporations. (There's also more than a whiff of paternalism in these "sin" taxes.) The taxes relied upon are comparatively easy to collect, and a VAT in particular is hard to evade, boosting tax compliance (Lindert 2021, Kenworthy 2020).

On the expenditure side, tilting toward spending on programs that develop children's capacities, with emphasis on children of low-income parents, is good for them and the rest of us as well over the course of their lives. Spending public funds on education, especially in ways that improve the across-the-board quality of primary schools, and on high-quality pre-Kindergarten and after-school care, is expenditure of the type best supported by empirical evidence that it improves the life prospects of recipients (Heckman 2006).

But even setting to the side this best-supported type of public spending, we find that the changing levels and overall amounts of state social spending in now-wealthy countries since 1890 do not correlate with shifting overall levels and rates of increase of GDP (Lindert 2021, 157–60). Nor do careful attempts to investigate cause and effect support the idea that using state power to help the poor ends up killing or wounding the goose that lays the golden eggs of increased prosperity across generations. State spending on social insurance that benefits the sick and injured, the elderly and frail, and those out of work, thus successfully helping people, also helps them be more productive. A caveat here is that aid to the young does more in this vein than pensions to the elderly, and countries that channel their public spending too much toward income support for the elderly, especially if the tilt is toward the elderly nonpoor, might benefit from following the example of the Nordic welfare states, which avoid this excessive tilt. (I admit, this formulation begs the question, how much tilt is excessive, which needs further discussion.)

There are further explanations for the apparent fact that high levels of public social spending are socially beneficial. State administration of health care insurance, mandating insurance for all and providing assurance of good care for all, turns out on the available evidence to be more cost-effective, delivering better health outcomes per dollar spent, than the alternative of leaving health insurance to private provision on the basis of individuals' capacity and willingness to pay for it. State policies that facilitate women's taking employment and sticking with their careers and mixing it up with men on equal terms in the labor market advance feminist goals and in doing so benefit all of us who enjoy goods and services produced by more competent and assiduous occupants of economic roles. Universal provision of benefits conditional only on need can, in some circumstances, lower administrative costs of provision of benefits, by reducing bureaucracy that would be needed to distinguish, among needy applicants for aid, those who are truly deserving, by prevailing standards, from those deemed undeserving. Active labor market policies that provide retraining to those lacking skills now in demand and help in matching available jobs and qualified applicants, and nudges to those dismayed by the job market, when done right, can be effective in promoting employment (Card, Kluve, and Weber 2018). Moderate labor and product market regulation, where "moderate" basically means avoiding regulation that increases bureaucratic red tape and slows or blocks completion of mutually beneficial private transactions, increasing their cost, without achieving compensating benefits, is also part of the mix of policies pursued by successful welfare states. Finally, a democratic legislature's judicious, limited restrictions of people's liberty for their own good (picture Arneson choosing between a lunch of fentanyl or vegetables) and nonrational manipulation of their decision making (picture emotion-triggering public health advertisements) can be part of a mix of public policies that boost equality-weighted well-being on the whole, even though some individuals would be better off without the restrictions and manipulations and left to choose on their own.

Equality Between Men and Women

For several decades, women's employment rates compared to men's have been high in the Nordic countries and much higher than in Southern European countries, where social policies and social norms support a family model in which the male spouse is the breadwinner and the female wife is responsible for childrearing and household management. This surely matters. "Several studies show that the share of household income a husband or wife contributes positively affects their share of private consumption goods" (Browning and Bonke 2006, cited in Folbre 2009). More broadly, if women lack labor force attachment, they will tend to have less bargaining power in the family, and generally will be subordinate to some man.

As far back as 1985, women's employment rate in Sweden was almost 80% of men's. The Nordic countries have implemented policies that aim to encourage women who give birth to maintain a career. In Denmark, a woman who gives birth is entitled to a year's paid parental leave with a guarantee that she will be able to resume her job after that leave. Subsidized, affordable state-provided child care is available for toddlers; almost 90% of Danish children aged one to two and 98% of children aged three to five are enrolled in child care. Those children enrolled in pre-school child care in the Nordic nations spend more hours per week on average in care than the children likewise enrolled in other nations.

Another bit of evidence is the Gender Inequality Index (GII) that the United Nations Development Program calculates for each nation. The GII is a measure of women's status in terms of health and longevity, education, and labor market. Denmark, Sweden, Norway, and Finland year after year are almost always among the top ten. You might suspect that the issues salient for gender equality in poor countries may differ from those most relevant for the assessment of wealthy countries. On similar measures crafted specifically for wealthy countries, ratings for Nordic countries are also superior. Along the same line, we might point to the extent to which women are represented in parliaments and have emerged as political leaders in wealthy countries.

There are wrinkles in this picture. The employment rates capture having a job versus not having a job, but women incline to part-time employment more than men, though this trend is not pronounced in Nordic countries (with the exception of Norway). Women with full-time employment work on the whole work fewer hours per week than men (Gregory 2009), and fewer hours in Nordic countries than in the United States. Women's employment in the Nordic countries, as in almost all wealthy nations, is concentrated in traditional female occupations such as nursing and teaching. Women's employment pooling in traditional pink-collar occupations tends to dampen their wages. However, the gender wage gap (the difference between the median earnings of men and women divided by men's median earnings) is lower in the Nordic countries than in the United States, Canada, and other countries with comparably large women's labor force participation (the gender wage gap tends to be low in countries where women's labor force participation rate is low).

Another aspect of gender equality is the extent of men's contributions to housework and childrearing activity, compared to women's, in married and cohabiting couples in which one member is a man, one a woman. If the employment of women in couples increases, but women continue to do a constant share—the lion's share—of housework and childrearing, it is hard to discern progress toward equality. In fact, since the 1980s, there has been some progress toward equal sharing of paid employment and self-employment, childrearing, and housework, throughout European countries and some others, but especially in Denmark, Norway, and Sweden, and everywhere mainly confined to college-educated couples. Among these couples, women with labor force attachment are spending more time taking care of their children than in the past, and are spending much less time doing housework, whereas men's time spent with their children has increased and time spent doing housework has budged upward only modestly (Esping-Andersen 2009). The main shift toward equality has arisen from reductions in women's time spent on housework.

It would be glib to extrapolate the limited progress made in some countries toward justice between men and women in family life into the further future and declare victory for the cause. The obstacles to further progress are large. But Scandinavian countries, with some others, have led the way.

Equality Between Young and Old

If a society favors the old over the young (or the reverse) over long stretches of time, the individuals favored at one stage of their lives would be disfavored at another stage, so this favoring has little inherent tendency to make individuals more unequal in their lifetime well-being levels. It might seem that insofar as equalizing lifetime well-being of persons is what we should seek, equality between age groups should be of no concern from an egalitarian standpoint.

This is wrong for at least three reasons. First, not everyone lives to old age, so policies that steadily over time favor the old are favoring people who are already advantaged compared to those who die young. Second, policies that channel social spending toward the young in ways that promote their productive skills and long-term health promote economic growth. This greater prosperity over time, in turn, enables society to improve people's lifetime well-being and, with political will, shift some of it in an equalizing direction. Third, there are cohort effects. For example, when the average age of workers is rising, there can be crowding at the top of the job market, and difficulty for young workers at that time to get good entry-level jobs and advance in their careers throughout their working lives (Bianchi and Paridisi 2024).

The Nordic countries do well at channeling social spending, and specifically pro-poor spending, toward children and youths, so that young people get a good start in life. Getting a slow start, for example, by seeking and not securing employment in early adulthood, tends to have negative effects on labor force attachment, income, and other outcomes of concern over the life course. OECD Stats 2018 (cited in Jensen 2021) shows the percentage of NEETS (not in education, employment, or training) of those aged 20–24 in Denmark, Norway, and Sweden to be lower for both men and women than in the United States and about three times lower than in Italy. Another indicator from the same source is that the percentage of citizens aged 25–34 with a college degree is about the same in Denmark and Sweden as in the United States and slightly higher in Norway (close to 50%) and in these countries twice as high as the corresponding percentage for Italy.

Besides educating and training the young, keeping markets competitive and unburdened by excessive regulation that makes it costly for firms to shrink their workforce in response to changing market conditions helps young people find employment. Adjusting state-provided retirement pensions so they do not absorb too great a fraction of GDP as the fraction of the population that is elderly increases, as is happening now in the Nordics and other wealthy societies, is also required for fairness between young and old. On both of these fronts, the NSD countries perform well.

Nuances, Shadings, Limits

There are nuances and some dark shadings in this rosy overview of progress toward equality in the Nordic countries that plausible moral principles should endorse. While highlighting progress in equality between men and women, the overview says nothing about equality between other salient social groups. Until recently, the

Nordic populations have been largely homogeneous in terms of race, ethnicity, and religion, and denial of equal treatment has not been at the foreground of discussion. That's changing. Increasing migration has made Nordic countries more diverse, and increasing pressure for migration makes rising intolerance a big challenge going forward.

A plausible indicator and component of quality of life is life expectancy at birth. A closely related indicator is healthy life expectancy—what is the average number of years of living without disabling health impairment that one can expect in one's country at birth? For long periods following World War II, Iceland, Sweden, and Norway led the world in life expectancy. As of a 2017 Global Burden of Diseases Study, the Nordics on average have higher life expectancy than the average of high-income countries across the world, but no longer are world leaders, and Finland (for men) and especially Denmark (for men and women) are lagging. Alcohol overuse in Finland and Denmark among males, and high rates of smoking among men and women in Denmark, lie behind their lower life expectancies. Of particular concern is that "gaps in life expectancy by socioeconomic status are larger in the Nordic states than in many less egalitarian societies" (Knudsen et al. 2019, e665). Some discount in this negative appraisal may be appropriate insofar as premature deaths lowering life expectancy in Nordic countries below what is elsewhere achieved are concentrated among those over 65, and for most of us, the main determinants of our lifetime well-being will be made in early and middle adulthood while we are in our healthy prime.

If we give some credit to Nordic states for fostering a culture that promotes gender equality, we should also assign some discredit to them insofar as they fail to promote a culture that boosts life expectancy and healthy life expectancy, especially for their less advantaged citizens. Recall that we are engaged in defending NSD by showing that the countries that implement it score high on a wide variety of indicators of better quality of life for their members and especially for their worse-off members. Showing that builds a plausible case that NSD does better at maximizing equality-weighted well-being than alternative political and economic arrangements. Life expectancy along with healthy life expectancy is a plausible rough indicator of good quality of life attained over people's complete lives. So is reducing the gap between the life expectancy of members of society with high socioeconomic status (SES) and the life expectancy of those with low SES, or more simply bringing about gains in life expectancy specifically for the latter.

In the 1950s through the 1970s, when Nordic welfare states made some of their greatest advances, boosting the income and providing basic insurance and assistance to the more disadvantaged members of society were good strategies for boosting their well-being as indicated by many proxy measures. New challenges have emerged. With rising life expectancy, and an aging population, there is a need to raise the retirement age past 65, to keep pension plans fiscally sound. But this is problematic if large numbers of citizens develop disabilities that prematurely rule out continued work. Carsten Jensen reports that presently nonskilled workers in Denmark "are only active in the labour market for an average of 22.3 years" (2023, 42). Raising the retirement age across the board is problematic in another way if some will expectably enjoy significantly fewer years of retirement before dying compared to the rest of the population. In the current state of medical progress, the low-lying fruit, picking which will boost healthy life expectancy, is found in behavior conducive to good health. The familiar components of this behavior include refraining from smoking, avoiding excessive alcohol intake, exercising more, eating a healthy diet heavy on fruits and vegetables, avoiding avoidable obesity, and maintaining social ties. These behaviors are disproportionately taken up by the more educated and already better off. Moreover, if those with more education and income and social status have health problems, they are on average more adept than the rest of us at taking advantage of the health care available to all in a universalistic health care and social safety net scheme.

Are there good public policy responses to such new challenges? Attempts to induce behavior change against culturally entrenched habits might seem a dubious endeavor, not only unlikely to succeed but involving hard trade-offs. Public service announcements might just annoy the target audience. Coercing individuals for their own good is both morally controversial and often experienced as obnoxious by those coerced. For some of us, sticking with our bad habits will be the overall prudent course, in which case government intrusion will expectably make us worse off.

However, consider legal prohibitions of drugs such as heroin and cocaine. If the benefits of these prohibitions sufficiently outweigh their moral costs, they can be justified even if some exceptionally good choosers, perhaps along with others, would be better off with no prohibition in place. If some paternalistic criminal law prohibitions can be justified, similar less coercive policies employing less coercive carrots and sticks can also be acceptable, even if paternalism is usually a bad bet (Mill 1859). Notice also that some alcohol control measures might be justifiable by appeal to preventing harm to others, not the drinker, as in alcohol-fueled car crashes.

Challenges can sometimes be overcome, and difficult trade-offs successfully balanced. With respect to efforts by government to induce healthy behaviors, there is the positive example of efforts to curb smoking. Governments can give wide publicity to empirical facts linking smoking to an array of diseases, restrict smoking in bars and other public spaces where nonsmokers are exposed to tobacco smoke, require warning labels on cigarette packages, and so on. One policy that has greater effect on those with less income is to raise the price of tobacco products by taxing sales (Mackenbach 2019, 110).

Another feature of an attractively egalitarian society as we intuitively conceive of it is equality of opportunity to flourish, which would obtain if all members of society have the same chances of flourishing independently of their unchosen circumstances. An observable indicator of likely progress is social mobility, the degree to which children's occupational status or income is correlated with the occupational status or income of their parents. Until recently, what has been studied is the average correlation between father's occupation (or income) and sons' occupation or income. Parents' educational attainments might also be compared to children's income or occupational status or educational attainments.

The Nordic countries show mixed performance on social mobility. Children from low SES families in Nordic countries have greater chances of rising up in income and occupation than similar children in wealthy countries with less generous welfare states, especially the United States. But at the top, children from high SES families tend to stay high in income and occupation. In this connection, some speak of a glass floor protecting those born into privilege. Giacomo Corneo comments that compared to the United States and most other nations, recent studies reveal that in Sweden "the children of poor parents are more likely to break out of their earning stratum by earning more" but also that "the economic elite in Sweden is pretty impenetrable" (2017, 229, also Esping-Andersen and Cimentada 2018, and for another view, Heckman and Landerso 2022).

Self-Reported Assessments of Well-Being/Happiness

The *World Happiness Report*, an annual publication of the Sustainable Development Solutions Project of the United Nations, ranks each country in the world according to the results of a survey of a sample of its inhabitants. Each respondent is asked this question: "Please imagine a ladder, with steps numbered from 0 at the bottom to 10 at the top. The top of the ladder represents the best possible life for you and the bottom of the ladder represents the worst possible life for you. On which step of the ladder would you say you personally feel you stand at this time?" A worry is that people in different cultures might interpret the numbers on the scale differently, or differentially regard it as sophisticated to report a low number. There is some evidence that those at the bottom of the totem pole in highly stratified societies might regard it as a test of loyalty to superiors on whom they are dependent to report a high number.

Economist Jeffrey Sachs, coauthor of the Report, said in 2021 that "we find year after year that life satisfaction is reported to be happiest in the social democracies of northern Europe." Of course, the rankings do not provide any evidence that putting in place and sustaining social democracy on the Nordic model causes those countries' populations to report and, if the self-reports are accurate, have greater life satisfaction than other countries or than the Scandinavian countries themselves would have without such social democracy. The most the survey data show is that having NSD in place does not prevent the Scandinavian countries from performing well on this measure. Whether we should regard subjective well-being reports as a useful indicator at all of genuine well-being attained is a question I leave aside without discussion. It is intuitively plausible that it is at least a rough indicator.

Democratic Equality

Democratic politics in Scandinavian countries exhibits desirable features. One is that voter turnout is high. An established political science finding is that those who are not economically well off tend to participate less in democratic politics, and this effect appears to be stronger in less egalitarian countries. For example, a 2012 study of voting patterns in the United Kingdom and Sweden found that of those who say they find it very difficult to get by on their present income (this fraction of the citizenry being smaller in Sweden), only 20% in Sweden but 56% in the United Kingdom are nonvoters (European Social Survey Round 6 Data). Carsten Jensen (2021) reports that in recent national elections, "around 85 percent of eligible voters showed up at the ballot boxes in Denmark and Sweden, while 78 percent cast their votes in Norway. In the U.S., a low-equality country, only around 66 percent voted in the 2020 presidential election" (and only 56% in 2016). More broadly, voter turnout rates in the Scandinavian countries (and some others including New Zealand) have held steady and high for many years, in contrast to declining rates in many wealthy democracies. Low-income voters in Scandinavian countries report less cynicism about democratic politics than elsewhere. Trust in one's government and belief that voting results influence elected officials' behavior are not surprisingly associated with propensity to vote.

The more that low-income citizens do not vote, the less likely it is that elected officials will pay heed to their concerns. A reasonable conjecture is that a society's being more equal in significant ways increases the voting of lower-income voters, and this in turn makes it more likely that equality-favoring policies will be sustained.

High voter turnout might reflect, and advance, equal opportunity for political influence a bit. But the concern that nowadays wealth corrupts and undermines democratic politics has much more to do with the impact of great and increasing wealth at the top of the wealth distribution.

Wealth Compression

The Scandinavian countries do not seek to equalize wealth by taxes or other policies that strive to take away wealth from the very rich for redistributive purposes. However, it should be noted that the wealthiest persons in the United States are far wealthier than the wealthiest citizens of Scandinavian countries. These countries have rich people, but not ultra-rich.

Is inequality of wealth a problem? If society provides basic security and safety and social insurance, and access to acceptable steady employment with after-tax income that enables all to live decently well, is it a social justice problem that some people are filthy rich? No, suggests Lane Kenworthy (2022, 128). He acknowledges that the inequality is marbled with unfairness, since major causes of what makes people rich or poor are beyond their power to control. But this may reasonably not matter to us all that much. After all, it should not trouble me too much if others are better-looking than I am, or more intelligent, or better at sports, through no fault of my own.

We should question this equanimity in the face of great inequality of wealth. First, some clarification will help. From a welfarist egalitarian (WE) standpoint, downward transfer of money or other resources is at most contingently valuable and never in itself morally valuable. With small wealth and income, Arneson might drink beer and live well, and with larger wealth and income, he would use cocaine and heroin and live a worse life. Money and other general-purpose resources are, after all, resources, and only expectably improve one's life if used wisely.

But the present discussion reasonably assumes that, on the whole and on the average, people will live better if they have greater general-purpose resources such as money (on the effects of lack of resources on capability to function and live well, see Mullainathan and Shafir 2013, Shafir 2017). This will especially be so if society invests in the education and upbringing of children to facilitate their being able to reason well and make prudent choices (and conform to reasonable moral norms prevailing in their society). Also, sensible paternalism (reducing people's liberty against their will for their own good), limited in extent, can improve people's lives, even when we disagree about what's ultimately good. Moreover, it is reasonable to suppose that relative poverty matters for welfare. Those whose income is far below the median in their society cannot participate fully in the life of the community. They are to some extent outsiders. Hence, there is a tendency for equalizing money holdings to boost total well-being and, even more, equality-weighted well-being.

This tendency is limited. Equalizing money holdings by direct transfer likely has some tendency to dampen the incentives of those taxed and those who receive the tax funds, and at some point, this tendency will lessen productivity and economic growth for the current generation and future generations. Recall that high-spending welfare states avoid this result partly by implementing a package of policies that include direct transfer but are overall pro-growth and partly by not pushing equalization excessively far (Lindert 2004, 2021).

But there is reason to suspect that Nordics might not be getting the balance right and hewing to optimal policies from the WE perspective (see Saez and Zucman 2019). From a WE standpoint, great inequality of wealth is suspect on several counts. Possession of great wealth induces extravagant consumption: mansions, yachts, jewels, fancy clothes, armies of servants, you name it. Money spent in these ways would surely do enormously more to improve people's lives if transferred to less wealthy people, and even more so in priority-weighted moral calculation. (The money might well be even better spent on projects that will boost long-term sustainable economic development on a habitable planet. See discussion in Chapter II.5.)

Second, possession of enormous wealth by human beings, people like us, has a tendency to be character-deforming, and to induce the illusion you are just fundamentally far more worthy than other people. This is speculation, but reasonable speculation. Since the extremely wealthy are extremely influential, their character flaws have bad effects. Evidence suggests that in the United States, wealth controls political outcomes, voters are aware of this, and the resultant distortion of policy choices and voter cynicism are toxic (Gilens 2012, Page and Gilens 2017, Bartels 2018). The Nordic states by contrast are so far sustaining better functioning democracies (Jensen 2021). But if higher taxes on corporate profits (which mainly boost the holdings of the wealthy) and higher taxes on the wealthy can reduce the disparity in political influence between rich and poor without tipping the balance firmly to low growth, then we ought to enact such taxes, and the Nordic states are falling short by failing to do this. Heavy inheritance taxation, reducing transmission of wealth within families from generation to generation, stands out as a form of taxation of the wealthy that has small ill effects by dampening incentives to be productive, and good effects on equality of opportunity (Lindert and Williamson 2016, 259).

Is there a good reason to believe that the wealthy having more political influence than the rest of the citizenry gives rise to political decisions worse from the WE perspective than would be enacted if their influence decreased? Maybe the disproportionate power of the rich just increases the likelihood of wise decisions (Kogelmann 2023 suggests the wealthy, by pushing against unwise wealth redistribution, might exert benign influence). But it is not cynical to think that people tend to act somewhat in their narrow self-interest and greater political influence in the hands of a few tends to skew policy choice toward what is in the narrow self-interest of the few to the detriment of the poor. Peter Lindert calls attention to the puzzle that in the UK public funding on children's education lagged behind that of other industrializing countries, as did noneducational public spending on poverty relief. He suggests that the broad answer is that the UK elites that controlled politics after the 1832 narrow franchise expansion found it in their interest to steer away from public education and poverty relief, and that policies shifted only with expansion of the franchise to include women and the working class (Lindert 2004, ch. 35).

Marching under the banner of equalizing wealth need not involve abandonment of the social democratic commitment to class compromise, not class war. What is at issue here is an adjustment in the terms of fair compromise. Moreover, past some point, refraining from further equalization of wealth might work in favor of boosting equal opportunity for political influence (EOPI), insofar as leaving intact some power in the hands of the wealthy provides a counterweight against worse EOPI erosion arising from unchecked power in the hands of elected democratic officials, giving them opportunities to entrench their power in the direction of authoritarianism.

This is the case for compressing the distribution of wealth from a WE perspective. From a relational egalitarian (RE) standpoint, the arguments are different, but somewhat converge. The more priority the RE position assigns to EOPI, along with other basic liberties, over securing resources for all that will boost people's real freedom to achieve their life aims, the more the RE case for wealth equalization turns on its likely impact on EOPI fulfillment. John Rawls states flatly that a capitalist welfare state, which as he conceives of it makes no attempt to fulfill EOPI by curtailing the influence of wealth, cannot be just. Only (1) a property-owning democracy, which works to disperse "the ownership of wealth and capital, and thus to prevent a small part of society from controlling the economy, and indirectly, political life as well," or alternatively (2) a regime with state ownership of the bulk of the economy along with political democracy and liberal freedoms, could according to Rawls fulfill his proposed principles of justice (Rawls 2001, 135–40).

If, when, and to the degree that compression of wealth serves egalitarian justice, we should be for it. When I defend the ideal of NSDs, it is with the qualification that they might well be excessively tolerant of inequality of wealth.

5

Global Justice

From Within-Country Justice to Global Justice

So far we have examined the case for and against the institutions and practices of Nordic social democracy (NSD). The verdict is positive. Evaluated from the standpoint of egalitarian values—which I have urged are not narrowly sectarian or partisan, but just common-sense norms that all of us should embrace—the Nordic model rates a high grade. This package of arrangements does not deliver perfect social justice, but arguably comes tolerably close to delivering as much justice as we can reasonably expect to achieve, by any means, in our time, given our circumstances, including the circumstance that we humans are a particular evolved primate with inborn psychological propensities. For angels, maybe, a heavenly cooperative anarchy; for us humans, a social democratic state.

"Rates a high grade" registers a fuzzy vague judgment call, about which thoughtful people will disagree. I don't claim to have provided a knockdown argument.

The discussion to this point has ignored global justice issues. It addresses the question, what does social justice require for a single (affluent) political community considered in isolation from others.

However, if we step back and consider the effects on people all across the Earth of initiating and sustaining generous welfare state policies in wealthy countries, things look very different. Generous welfare state policies in wealthy countries, viewed in a global perspective, look to be redistribution merely between the very rich and the rich, since poor people in rich countries are in the upper half of people worldwide in terms of their wealth and income. Hence the

Debating Capitalism. Richard J. Arneson and Jason Brennan, Oxford University Press.
 DOI: 10.1093/9780190076467.003.0008

much admired Nordic welfare state policies do not significantly reduce global poverty (Weyl 2018) and are no big deal at all in terms of global justice. So one might hold.

The problem sharpens when some simple facts of global inequality are noted. The *World Inequality Report 2022* (Chancel 2022) indicates that in 2021, the bottom 50% of the world's population has 8.5% of total income measured in purchasing power parity, the next-higher 40% has 39.5%, and the top 10% has 52% of total income. *Income* here refers to income prior to tax and transfer but including what people get from pension benefits and unemployment compensation. Income so understood is highly unequally distributed across countries and also within countries. Almost none of the 50% of people with least income resides in rich countries in Europe and North America. Wealth is far more unevenly distributed. The same Report notes that the bottom 50% of world population, as of 2019, is responsible for 12% of carbon emissions, the next-higher 40% for 40%, and the top 10% for 48%.

Moreover, since people in poor countries work more hours per year than others, income inequality across the globe is less than inequality in income per hour spent working to earn it.

Add to these stark facts the further fact that to prevent catastrophic climate change, global greenhouse gas emissions must reduce to net zero in just a few years. Facilitating rapid economic growth and income growth in the countries in which half of the world's population with lowest incomes is housed would automatically massively increase their emissions, blocking progress toward net zero, unless the economic growth obtains simultaneously with switching in all countries to energy sources and technologies that emit net-zero greenhouse gasses.

It gets worse. Some theorists have urged that allowing and enforcing much greater freedom to migrate from country to country than current nation-states permit would be a uniquely feasible and effective way to promote prosperity and well-being worldwide and reduce or eliminate global poverty (Clemens 2011, also Milanovic 2019). Crudely put, in poor countries people are poor because where they currently live, their labor can only be deployed on scant and low-quality capital. Impoverished in Somalia, if I could move to say Chicago and seek employment there, I would either be able to work more productively on better capital, or at least work in a job whose wage is higher than I can now get due to generally higher productivity there. With completely open borders, it has been estimated that in the neighborhood of a third of the world's population would relocate, leading to massive economic gain. The gains would largely accrue initially to those who move to places where their incomes will increase, and also somewhat to those left behind, via remittances and higher wages. You might suspect that the gains of those who would migrate to rich countries in this scenario would come at the expense of a significant fraction of the present inhabitants of these rich countries, now forced to compete against newcomers. But if immigrants would contribute economically in ways that mainly complement rather than substitute for the skills and labor of the rich-country citizens, few of the latter would be harmed. Some say that closing borders as countries now do is foregoing huge gains—leaving "trillion dollar bills just lying on the pavement" (Clemens 2011, Pritchett 2010).

However, there appears to be a conflict between preserving or instituting generous welfare state policies of NSD in rich countries and fulfilling global justice duties by opening the doors—if not wide open, then much more so than at present—to temporary or permanent migrants from poor countries. One problem is that, at least in the short run, a massive influx of extremely poor migrants greatly increases the cost of generous welfare state programs and hence reduces the voters' willingness to pay for them. This problem could be avoided if rich countries admitted migrants only as long-term guestworkers lacking citizenship (and voting) rights along with government benefits to the poor that are restricted to citizens. But then social democratic equality among the country's inhabitants disappears. Either way, good-bye to NSD as we know it.

A second, perhaps more decisive problem is that generous welfare states arise and persist in countries with culturally and ethnically homogeneous populations. In these countries the "we" who pay most taxes identify with the "them" who are recipients and see them as part of "us." In countries with heterogeneous populations, not so much. We might wish this were not the case, but it seems to be the reality. The United States, with its history of slavery and continuing hostility of white people toward black people, along with stimulating but rancorous ethnic diversity, is a glaring illustration. Economists Alberto Alesina and Edward Glaeser (2004) report that about 50% of the difference between European and United States generosity toward the poor is racially based. They state, "A large literature has documented racial and ethnic antipathies, and a smaller literature has compellingly linked these feelings with hostility to welfare" (2004, 133–4, see also Gilens 1999).

Glen Weyl (2018) poses the challenge for global egalitarians who celebrate generous welfare state policies in rich countries provocatively by asking, which countries in the world do most on a per capita basis to reduce global poverty. The answer is that the oil-rich Gulf Coast Council (GCC) countries of the Middle East do most. They take in huge numbers of guestworkers from poor countries on a revolving door basis to do much of the labor, freeing their own well-off citizens from having to do much of it. The meager pay the guestworkers get exceeds what they could expect in their home countries, and much of this pay is transmitted back to impoverished relatives back home. No generous welfare state benefits flow to the guestworkers. Authoritarian and repressive regimes like Kuwait do more to alleviate global poverty than Scandinavian social democracies.

The challenge, simply put:

1. Global justice requires maximizing equality-weighted well-being of all people, not merely one's fellow countrymen.
2. To maximize the equality-weighted well-being of all people, not merely one's fellow countrymen, requires a major opening of national borders permitting many people all across the Earth to resettle in rich countries.

3. A major opening of national borders permitting many people all across the Earth to resettle in rich countries is incompatible with initiation and continuation of Nordic (generous) social democratic policies in rich countries.
4. Conformity with what global justice requires is incompatible with initiation and continuation of Nordic (generous) social democratic policies in rich countries.

This argument looks to be valid, so if we accept 1, 2, and 3, we must embrace the conclusion 4, and the euthanasia of NSD.

Let's consider whether there are grounds for rejecting one or more of premises 1–3 and defending the continuation (and strengthening) of NSD.

Premise 1 might be contested on various grounds. One is that people have special tie duties to the members of their own political society, which take priority, to some extent, over their duties of beneficence pressing them to help needy people everywhere across the globe.

Another is that if justice has an egalitarian character, what equality demands of us is to regard and treat those we interact with as equals (not maximizing some function of their well-being). We should relate as equals to all. In matters of governance, we relate as equals by practicing a true democracy in which all have equal opportunity to influence political decision-making. On the face of it, relational egalitarian justice, even if it has a wide global scope of application, can be satisfied without compressing the world's distribution of wealth across countries and peoples. Establishing and sustaining political democracy in a nation-state does not require great wealth. With true democracy in each country of the world, global relational egalitarian justice might be satisfied, even though across the globe, there remains huge inequality of wealth between economically better-off and worse-off countries.

In the same spirit, one might hold that the requirement to treat people as equals is conditional on having interaction with them and causal effects on them and holds more strongly as these increase. If people lived on separate islands and there was no inter-island interaction and nothing done on one island causally affected life on the other, no island inhabitants would be treating inhabitants of any other islands at all, and a fortiori none would not be treating anyone as less than equal. In our actual world, there is global interaction, and people's actions have effects beyond their national borders. But density of interaction, and magnitude of the effects of one's actions on others, are generally greater within borders rather than across them. A general requirement to treat all with dignity and respect, as equals, might require much more of us, with respect to fellow countrymen, than to foreigners.

But none of these gambits looks promising. If we ought to be welfarist egalitarians, then widening the scope of egalitarian concern requires boosting prosperity in poor countries and compressing the worldwide distribution of wealth and income. And widening the scope of egalitarian concern looks to be mandatory once you think about it.

Also, one might accept that we can have significant special tie personal obligations, to friends and family and colleagues, with whom we personally interact, without accepting that we can have similar special ties (and accompanying obligations) to those to whom we have anonymous impersonal relationships, such as fellow members of our own ethnic group or fellow citizens of our nation-state (Arneson 2016).

The upshot is that for purposes of this discussion, we should accept premise 1. Then we shall be studying the global justice objection to initiating and sustaining generous social democracy welfare state policies in the form in which it most strongly challenges that project.

It should be noted in particular that if social justice with global scope permits or requires the members of each separate political society to favor comembers in some way, via special tie duties, that will weaken the objection to NSD based on global justice. A relational egalitarian case could be made for partiality to fellow countrymen (Rawls 1999b). Living in a tolerably well-functioning state, one benefits from the cooperation of fellow citizens who steadily bear costs that provide important goods that fall like rain on all people within the state's borders. Without these goods, such as police protection, national defense, the rule of law, and protection of some basic moral rights, none of us would have good chances of living well. Treating cooperating fellow citizens as equals arguably requires reciprocating their good will, by cooperating and paying our fair share (Sangiovanni 2007).

However, there seem to be holes in this argument for partiality to fellow countrymen. First, the argument as stated does not support partiality to all conationals, just the willing cooperators among them, who may be few. Second, the claim that my cooperating to help someone generates a duty of payback presupposes I have a right to use the resources I devote to this cooperation at my discretion. If a strong antecedent global justice duty claims these resources, I lack a right to use them as I choose, including to help those living nearby in a way that would trigger a payback duty on their part. Third, when a member of a wealthy nation gets further benefits from the cooperation of fellow members of her society, it is plausible that she should reciprocate and join in the cooperation rather than free ride on their help, just using her resources for herself. But if instead she reciprocates by helping worse-off people in distant lands successfully cooperate in a similar way, benefiting as she has benefited, she is not really free riding. She is doing her bit in a wider cooperative scheme and bringing about greater priority-weighted well-being gains for people, as welfarist egalitarianism requires. Arguably doing *that* is treating people as equals. (If the local cooperative scheme is fragile, and her failing to join in would push the scheme past a tipping point and cause great harm by degrading the local cooperative scheme, an impartial cosmopolitan norm such as priority with global scope will agree, in this circumstance, doing one's bit for local cooperation is morally required (Arneson 2016). This line of thought pushes us back to accepting premise 1.

In contrast, premise 2 screams for rejection. First, open borders, or anything close to that, would be a huge disruptive transformation that might not deliver anything close to the huge benefit its advocates anticipate. Its overall economic consequences are unknown (Hanson 2009, Collier 2013). Some increase in migration into rich countries from present levels might well be beneficial, but how much increase?

Moreover, even if much more open borders would be beneficial if accepted, popular resistance to it in rich countries might well lead to backlash and bad consequences, overshadowing and eventually destroying these potential economic benefits.

Even more important, for rich countries and their inhabitants, global justice duties are duties not to harm and beyond that, involve beneficence, directed at poor country inhabitants. There will almost always be several alternative ways to satisfy any beneficence duties (Wellman 2008, 126–7). So even if opening borders to increased migration would be a very effective way to fulfill one's global justice duties, there will in actual and likely circumstances be others. For example, Norway could contribute to aid programs in Somalia, or provide expert advice or technological knowledge, or donate or loan capital, or give up some of its territory to refugees, or send troops to restore good order menaced by civil war. In particular, insofar as people are poor because their access to capital is scant and hence their labor is unproductive, this problem could be solved either by moving people to where the capital is or by moving capital to where the people are.

Complication: It's not access to capital alone, rather combined with good institutions and culture, that matters for the productivity of labor. This complicates, without undermining, the point being made.

But a serious objection looms, to the effect that if the conditions for sustained economic development are not present in a poor country, foreign aid will be useless and likely counterproductive for starting it, and if the conditions are already present, foreign aid is not needed (Alesina and Dollar 2000, Easterly 2001, Deaton 2013, chap. 7, also Deaton 2023). This objection points toward genuine difficulties, but perhaps not to a sharp dilemma (for some evidence, see Balboni et al. 2022). The trick is to channel aid to places where other conditions are in place that make it likely the aid will boost development, but not conditions that render such aid otiose. Also, given that institutions and culture certainly do matter, effective aid must be directed in ways that facilitate economic growth and poverty elimination by facilitating complementary institutional and cultural change.

In some situations, for some stretches of time, the best judgment may be that nothing can be done for now in some places where conditions are deplorable. Handing money to an entrenched dictator who gives no credible sign of becoming willing to put good policies in place would not help. For progress, all that is needed is that there are among poor countries some that can be helped effectively here and now.

A related objection points to history. We see examples of poor countries successfully nurturing economic development and becoming wealthier, but we see no unambiguous examples of foreign aid succeeding in nudging a poor country onto a path that leads it to successful development (Deaton 2013, 267–324).

In response, it is not as though history is littered with episodes in which rich countries altruistically aim at poor country development and take serious sustained well-calculated steps toward this goal, yet these episodes always go awry somehow. Countries use foreign aid to advance their own national interests such as gaining advantage in big-power rivalries. Since the aid is not aimed at altruistic goals, it is not mysterious that altruistic goals are not attained. So this history implies nothing about what a country that aimed to advance global justice could achieve. However, this response carries a cautionary implication. Campaigning successfully to induce a rich-country government to seek to do more to advance global justice does not guarantee that what it actually ends up doing will seek to advance global justice.

Yet another claim that doubts the potential effectiveness of even sincerely well-intended foreign aid rests on the observation that a state has vastly more power to control what happens within its borders, where it has a mostly effective monopoly on the use of force, than what happens outside its borders. The reply is simply that this broad observation holds sometimes, not always, and does not substitute for careful case-by-case analysis. After all, states often go to war, with huge impact for better or worse on large areas of the world outside their borders. In a globalized world, state actions other than war also often have a wide geographical impact.

If developed countries can fulfill global justice duties without adopting policies that verge on open borders, should they do so? There is a moral gain if people in rich countries living under NSD fulfill their global justice duties by moving—or better, donating—capital to people in poor countries rather than by facilitating large increases of in-migration of people from poor countries. In the migration scenario, the costs to NSD citizens, via collapse or erosion of generous welfare state practices, will be borne preponderantly by the less well off fraction of these citizens. Moreover, if immigration causes social disruption in the host country, its negative effects will likely fall on less affluent citizens of these host countries who live in neighborhoods where poor immigrants cluster. (This remains true even if the ungracious host country residents are morally at fault for the discord and squabbling.) In the capital transfer alternative scenario, the costs are shouldered more by rich than by poor citizens in rich countries, provided that the taxes that fund these costs are set to secure this result. The second scenario is more fair according to welfarist egalitarian justice standards with global scope.

Also, we should acknowledge that "open borders" does not lie within the politically feasible set of immigration policies that might be chosen. Rich-country voters will not vote for it, and in wealthy nondemocracies, dictators will not impose it. The same holds for complete fulfillment of a rich country's global justice duties, when these are interpreted along the very demanding lines of cosmopolitan welfarist egalitarianism. Attention shifts to what can be attained. For any politically feasible degree of global justice duties fulfillment on the part of a rich country, attained by opening its borders to large-scale migration, there will be a more fair strategy that the country can follow that attains that same degree of global justice duty fulfillment. The alternative strategy involves capital transfer from rich to poor countries along with ancillary measures. Rather than deny that rich countries in current times are bound by very demanding global justice duties, we should favor equitable sharing of their burdens, placing a good part of them onto the shoulders of better-off members of wealthy societies.

To be sure, if immigration that involves largely the entry of poor people from poor countries is a highly cost-effective means by which a rich country can fulfill its global justice obligations, in principle, the immigration-friendly policy can be combined with policies that compensate its worse-off citizens so that the costs of global justice fulfillment are equitably shared among all rich-country citizens. The strategy for advancing global justice fulfillment that includes welcoming members of the global poor as migrants then would attain a greater degree of fulfillment while imposing less sacrifice on host country citizens than alternative strategies that are not immigration-friendly in this way. But if the costs of the immigration-friendly policy arise by way of social discord and disruption, lessening of social trust and solidarity, and erosion and collapse of generous welfare state policies, such compensation may be in practice unobtainable.

This line of thought will attract objections. An obvious one is that significant donations of capital (or the equivalent) from Scandinavian countries to the global poor would itself conflict with maintenance of generous NSD policies. The response is that we should distinguish generous and ample NSD policies. With lower tax money available to fund those policies, there will be some penny-pinching, but this is compatible with maintaining their generous egalitarian and pro-poor tilt. Another worry is that the capital transfer being envisaged would clearly dampen economic growth in NSD countries, but this effect should be offset by rising growth rates in poor country recipients of this aid. And if economic development policies are successful, they need not be sustained for an indefinitely long time.

What if, within some range between fully open and fully closed, opening borders to migrants is more effective at boosting priority-weighted well-being worldwide than alternative measures? This may be, but by sacrificing more, to get as good an outcome, citizens of a wealthy country determined to keep borders closed can still fulfill global justice duties. A qualification here is that pursuing global justice by extremely inefficient means might leave insufficient resources to fulfill other binding moral duties even if global justice duties are satisfied.

If premise 2 is false, what is there to say about 3? It's speculative, and contestable. No law of physics absolutely rules out the possibility that ethnically and culturally heterogeneous groups of people might live together amicably, with wide social trust and solidarity, yielding a stable voting majority for generous welfare state policies. After all, in some places and times, heterogeneous societies thrive. Robert Putnam (2007) surmises that rich societies are becoming and will become increasingly heterogeneous, and that in the long run, people in heterogeneous societies will learn to live together cooperatively and amicably. As of 2021, "Almost 20 percent of all Swedish inhabitants are foreign born, with numbers somewhat lower in Denmark and Norway" (Jensen 2021). However, if premise 2 is false, the argument to the pessimistic conclusion regarding the compatibility of fulfilling global justice, construed as having wide scope of application, and initiating and maintaining NSD, anyway falls to the ground—regardless of the truth or falsity of 3.

Return to the question, does compressing the distribution of income and life prospects among the global rich pale into insignificance by comparison with compressing it across the entire global population? There are reasons to support a No answer. Recall the prioritarian view that getting a benefit to a person is morally more valuable, the worse off the person would otherwise be in lifetime well-being. Assuming that very roughly those with higher income will tend to have overall better lives, a transfer of a benefit without loss from the very best off to someone at the very bottom of the world distribution will be morally more valuable than transferring the benefit to someone higher of the distribution, but a transfer from best off to someone in the middle of the distribution still brings about significant moral gain (how much depends on what weight attaches to priority for the worse off). The welfarist egalitarian gains that NSD sustains are then not, morally speaking, small potatoes, even though it is true that bringing it about that the lives of the global poor improve, even at some considerable cost to better offs, is morally more important.

Furthermore, it should not be assumed without question that the higher one's disposable income, the better one's life goes for one.

Relative poverty, having less income than others, when it grows high, tends to result in social exclusion, not being able to participate fully as a valued member in the life of one's community, which can make one's life go worse. On the other side, having far greater income than others, beyond some point, can bring about bads including distracting snobbery, false feelings of superiority, and status competitions that are unproductive with respect to conditions conducive to well-being increases overall, broadly shared across people, in the long term.

From another angle, with an eye on white US citizens with no more than a high school education, the economists Anne Case and Angus Deaton (2021) observe that by several indicators, including life expectancy, their quality of life has deteriorated in recent years. Deaton (2023) floats the conjecture that by sensible fine-grained assessment of their overall conditions of life, many of them are appropriately classified as below the top half of global inhabitants. Assume that his conjecture (if correct) holds only for Americans, and not for citizens of Scandinavian welfare states, who do not exhibit nearly as much of the signs of troubled lives as the group Deaton is characterizing. Nonetheless, if generous welfare state policies or some equivalent factor is needed to keep members of the working class of rich countries from being aptly classified within the broad global poor, this would signal that the collapse of NSD institutions where they now exist should register by proper global justice accounting as a big deal.

In this discussion, "well-being" has been so far an unspecified placeholder. To give welfarist egalitarianism a fair hearing, the idea of well-being (what in itself makes a person's life go better for her) should be accorded its most plausible interpretation. I suggest an objective list conception, according to which there are things such as pleasure, friendship, love, and achievement, such that the more your life contains these things, the better your life is going for you, independently of your attitudes and opinions on this matter.

It might seem that this convoluted defense of rich-country citizens voting to close up borders in order to preserve prospects for initiating and sustaining generous welfare state policies fails, because the voters will end up practicing morally objectionable discrimination when enacting the border control policies under review. Given the changing demographics in rich countries with generous welfare state policies that will result in an increasing fraction of the population becoming elderly in coming years, a complete halt to migrants will put increasing strain on the capacity of their governments to keep financing generous welfare state policies. The result would be erosion of welfare state policies generous to the poor. Instead significant numbers of migrants must be admitted. But to avoid the social disruptions we have described, these migrants must be culturally, religiously, ethnically, racially close to the characteristics predominant in the current host country population. In near-term empirically likely circumstances, policies that would sustain NSD will involve morally objectionable discrimination.

Reply 1. In the case at hand, voters are disfavoring the members of a salient social group seeking entry in order to avoid social disruption that will damage or destroy NSD policies that advance local justice while fulfilling nonlocal justice duties to aid the global poor in other ways. Arguably it is not morally objectionable to preserve locally just NSD by this means.

Objection to Reply 1. The reference to "social disruption" here is disingenuous. "We NSD citizens expect to be inhospitable to racially/culturally alien newcomers, leading to social disruption and allied harms." This claim is not an acceptable ground for exclusion. It's a good reason to overcome the disposition to wrongful inhospitality.

Reply to Objection. Suppose our family ought pro tanto to invite Sally to dinner, to give her a good time, but if we do so, my father will inevitably and unavoidably misbehave and spoil the party. Then all things considered, we should not invite Sally to dinner. This is reasonable coping with my father's boorishness, not excusing it. Same goes with the suggested denial of entry to would-be migrants whom some of our fellow countrymen (wrongly) regard as undesirable. Or better, change the example so that the family has many members, and although each of us could refrain from inhospitality to a possible invited guest, the temptation to inhospitality is large for each of us, and the chances that a sufficient number of us could resist the temptation to spoil the party are too small to warrant issuing the invitation. The revised example better fits the decision problem the rich country deciding whether to admit migrants who are members of the global poor.

It should be acknowledged, the line of reasoning to which I appeal, in the mouths of those who assert it, often has a bad smell. "We cannot do this otherwise morally required thing, because if we attempted to do it, some of us would sabotage the undertaking, making the situation morally worse." This was vigorously asserted against proponents of civil rights advances against white supremacy in the United States in the 1950s and 60s by white people who benefited from the continuation of racial injustice, and whose judgment, in hindsight, looks to have been corrupted by their fondness for these wrongful privileges. Nonetheless, it is sometimes true that implementing some proposals intended to reduce injustice, for now, would actually increase the injustice, or be unavoidably accompanied by sufficient bads to justify rejecting the proposals.

NSD for Rich Countries Only, or for All Countries?

NSD might be deemed a luxury good that only a rich society can afford. On reflection, this thought looks to be wrong. "Indonesia and China are now more developed . . . than Britain was in 1948 when it started its monumental National Health Service [NHS]. The Scandinavian countries built key components of their welfare states . . . before the Second World War, at an even lower level of economic development" (Fleurbaey et al. 2018, 158). Being wealthy at the level of the richest countries of the world is not a prerequisite for building institutions and practices of NSD. In a similar way, being of Nordic ethnicity is not required for a nation to commit itself to "Nordic" social democracy (Kenworthy 2020, 72–93). Even should it be the case that cultural homogeneity—being alike in ethnicity, religion, and language—makes it easier to foster the solidarity and national unity required for construction of NSD in a country (Alesina and Glaeser 2004), there might be feasible substitutes for this homogeneity in countries where it is lacking. One possibility is that shared history of the right sort, shared commitment to values that dispose the valuers to social democratic arrangements, or some combination of these two ingredients of social unity might suffice to generate sustained support of a generous and inclusive welfare state. Another possibility is that some form of class solidarity across a heterogeneous population might supply the social glue that facilitates a transition to NSD.

Yet another possibility is that in some cases, where ethnic strife is entrenched and may look to be intractable, state borders can be redrawn, and where necessary, populations humanely resettled, to facilitate solidarity and national unity in each separate state. The idea is that national borders should be drawn, and when need be, redrawn, to facilitate the greatest reachable overall fulfillment of global justice over the long run.

All else equal, the moral justice reasons that demand effective pro-poor policies are stronger in a poor and developing country than in a rich and developed one. The poor are poorer, not only in access to resources but in life prospects, in a poor country. The priority-weighted expected moral value of getting an extra dollar into someone's hands, as a means to boosting her welfare, is greater, the less cash she would have absent receipt of this benefit. Moreover, as the very rich in poor countries come to have wealth and income levels close to those of the very rich in rich countries, the moral disvalue of taking a dollar from rich-in-poor-country may tend to be about the same as taking a dollar from rich-in-rich-country.

In this connection, we should distinguish generous and ample welfare state benefits. Whether a welfare state achieves a Nordic level of generosity is not fixed by the monetary amount of its outlays but on this monetary amount relative to its Gross Domestic Product per citizen and more generally its level of economic development. Generous policies sustained by a poor nation may likely not provide ample benefit levels per person. That will vary with circumstances. But generous less than ample policies can deliver large boosts to social justice. In particular, policies that increase the marketable skills of the poor along with helping them find productive employment that utilizes their skills will tend to generate long-term sustainable justice gains. It would be wrong to make a fetish of the specific NSD approach (for broadly egalitarian doubts, see Bowles 2012). About a dozen rich countries currently channel 20% of their Gross Domestic Product into social spending (25% if public education spending is included). France, Austria, Belgium, and Germany are included among the top seven spenders, along with the Scandinavian countries of Sweden, Denmark, and Finland. (Norway's offshore oil wealth lowers its social spending/GDP ratio a bit, putting it toward the bottom of the 12.) These high-spending welfare states attain several egalitarian outcomes, although the Southern European members of this group (Italy, Spain, and Portugal) along with Germany do less well at boosting women's employment and gender equality, and some non-Nordic welfare states arguably tilt too heavily toward pensions for the elderly (and even more, *nonpoor* elderly), and France appears to have excessive labor market regulation in relation to any discernible benefits gained from it.

It should also be noted that some Asian countries, notably Taiwan and South Korea and to some degree Japan, manage the feat of sustaining rather low post-tax post-transfer income inequality without large tax and transfer policies, indeed without much public social spending. Their pre-tax pre-transfer income distribution is more equal than that of many countries. The features of their economies that induce this result may not be replicable in other settings, but their existence is a reminder that policies that result in greater pre-tax pre-transfer income equality may be an important component of reasonable egalitarian regimes.

On the expenditure side of tax and transfer redistribution, poor countries tend to have less state capacity for executing complex transfer policies, though the degree to which this is so varies widely across poor states. This state capacity deficit may in some cases boost the strength of the argument for an administratively simple transfer scheme such as an unconditional basic income (UBI) in poor countries, rather than the more complex schemes characteristic of NSD (Bannerjee and Duflo 2019). But this point equally increases the moral reasons for rich countries to contribute to facilitating an increase in poor countries state capacity when ways to do this present themselves (Collier 2008).

NSD would be a morally desirable set of social arrangements for any country that can pull off the trick of building it. It does not follow that this trick is easy to pull off, or even that it is possible in any currently poor country. In the Scandinavian countries, a strong form of social democracy arose due to a constellation of historical contingencies. This exact mix of historical contingencies is not exportable, and contingencies that give an equivalent causal push may not be ready to hand. Nonetheless, when we widen our gaze and consider what would contribute to global justice, pushing toward NSD wherever we ourselves live is revealed to be part of what we owe to others. Encouraging and facilitating the development of NSD in other countries are also important parts (but not the entirety) of what we owe to others.

This injunction to support and encourage applies to people everywhere, but with special force to citizens of countries that are rich and powerful today. In this sense, cosmopolitan global justice affirms NSD for all, in our time. We should all be seeking to bring about a world in which all have good chances of living in a "socialist hellhole, like Denmark."

PART III
BRENNAN

1

An Easy Choice

Open Borders or Social Democracy?

The social democratic capitalist societies of Australia, North America, Asia, and Europe have highly restrictive immigration regimes. They use immigration quotas and punitive labor regulations to exclude foreign workers, especially poor and unskilled workers, from their markets.

These restrictions profoundly harm the world's poorest people. They also harm the world's richest people, though far less. Why, then, do the social democracies restrict immigration?

Many politicians believe restrictions protect domestic citizens' high incomes from competition. This belief is probably mistaken, as I'll discuss below.

They also believe that they must choose between open borders or providing an expansive welfare state for current residents. They choose the latter.

They choose wrong. If we must choose between open borders or social democratic welfare states, open borders win, and win by a mile. It's not even a close competition, especially from a left-wing point of view.

The surprising upshot is that a more laissez-faire capitalist system would also be a much more equal system that better served the world's poor. Capitalist markets want to be more egalitarian. They want to enrich the world's poor. But modern social democracies and modern social democrats won't let them. Social democrats immiserate the global poor and push policies that preserve global inequality and poverty.

Debating Capitalism. Richard J. Arneson and Jason Brennan, Oxford University Press.
 DOI: 10.1093/9780190076467.C03.0010

The Speech

Imagine the next presidential campaign is in full swing. Presidential hopeful Donald Bernard—nickname DB—holds rallies before his fawning fans. Bono, Ariana Grande, Taylor Swift, and Bon Iver endorse him. College students wear his face on T-shirts. His bumper stickers adorn Subarus and pickup trucks alike.

Imagine that at one rally, DB declares:

> The problem with our economy is that the people at the very top do much better than the people who are merely *near* the top. In this new economy, the top 0.1% are enjoying tremendous growth while the top 15% see stagnation. Our economy is rigged!
>
> I will make it fair. When I'm president, the top 0.1% will share their income with the top 15%. The top 0.1% pay their fair share of taxes for the benefit of the top 15%. The economy will serve everyone in the top 15%, not just billionaires and CEOs at the very top.

After the speech, a puzzled economist asks DB, "What about the bottom 85%? A large number of peer-reviewed economics papers in leading journals show that while some of your policies will help some people in the top 15%, those same policies will greatly harm the bottom 85%, especially the people at the very bottom."

DB scoffs, "Those aren't *my* people. I don't represent *them*. I don't care about *them*."

I wouldn't call DB a humanitarian, an egalitarian, or someone deeply concerned with social justice. If we put his philosophy in slogan form, it would look like this:

> "Let's tax and redistribute from the ultra rich to the merely rich . . . at the expense of the genuinely poor!"
>
> "Social justice for the top 15% . . . at the expense of everyone else!"

DB is a fiction, but these attitudes are widespread. Most social democrats think this way, even if they don't quite admit it to themselves or their supporters. In fact, most real-life social democratic politicians—and the intellectuals who supply them with arguments—support policies that will harm the bottom 85% in order to help the top 15%.[1] The big twist is that the rich top 15% are citizens inside their own national borders, while the poorer bottom 85% are foreigners outside their borders.

The slogan "Social justice for the top 15% at the expense of the 85%" sounds awful and evil *inside* a single country. But if the richer 15% live in your country and the poorer 85% live elsewhere, suddenly most people find these ideas acceptable and admirable. Most people think there is some moral magic about national borders. They are willing to implement policies that predictably harm the poor so long as the poor carry different passports.

My Thesis

I will now argue that all people have a right to immigrate freely.[2] Foreign citizenship should not be a barrier to taking a job, or renting or buying a home, in another country. It should be nearly as easy to move between countries as it is to move within them.

I am uncertain how much we must choose between open borders or social democracy, because I am unsure how much of the social democratic welfare state can be sustained with open borders. As I write this, it seems the Nordic welfare states seem to think they must choose—Denmark in particular is radically reducing the amount of immigration it allows and is actively working to break up immigrant enclaves inside the country. Swedish and Norwegian politics frequently speak of an immigration crisis, and the laws are changing to be less permissive.

However, if we must choose, many of the very moral principles that supposedly support social democracy seem to favor open immigration of economic migrants. The case for choosing open borders

[1] In technical language, all of them favor this de re, and some, like Bernie Sanders or Donald Trump, favor it de dicto as well.

[2] To be more precise, even if, say, doctors should have a medical license before being allowed to practice medicine, my point is that a person's *nationality* should be no barrier.

over social democracy is overwhelming. As economist Bryan Caplan says, open borders is the liberal, libertarian, egalitarian, humane, economically efficient way to double world product.[3]

Many supposed champions of social justice—including socialist politicians like Bernie Sanders and self-described left-wing theorists such as Stephen Macedo and Seyla Benhabib—oppose free immigration and open borders. They think social democratic welfare states are unsustainable and incompatible with increased immigration. They say open borders would undermine social democratic solidarity. They say we must protect our fellow citizens from competition from genuinely poor foreign workers.

The extant research on this issue does not much support these ominous claims. However, even if the research is mistaken, it's hardly a left-wing or progressive idea to favor policies that hurt the genuinely poor in order to enhance the incomes of the relatively rich people.

Social Democracies Ensure World Markets Favor Capital over Labor

The world labor market is rigged to favor capital over labor. Surprisingly, one reason it's rigged is that modern social democratic societies are insufficiently laissez-faire.

Let's illustrate the basic mechanism with a hypothetical example. Imagine the only way the indigent can earn a living is to sell strawberries to the wealthy. Imagine that the international community creates two laws:

1. Strawberry sellers are forbidden to travel in search of a better deal. They must stand still and wait for customers to approach them.
2. Strawberry buyers may travel and buy strawberries anywhere.

[3] In person.

These rules would make the strawberry market uncompetitive. A competitive market, in the technical sense, is a market in which individual buyers and sellers have no extra bargaining power. Prices are determined entirely by supply and demand. Such laws would help rich, mobile strawberry buyers—who are free to search for the best deal—to exploit poor, immobile strawberry sellers—who are stuck having to take whatever deals come their way.

This is analogous to the world labor market. Financial instruments, money, information, capital, factories, may move easily across borders. Poor, unskilled laborers may not. Factories owners may build sweatshops in poor countries in search of cheap labor. Laborers may not cross borders to rich countries in search of high wages. Social democratic restrictions on immigration rig the system in favor of capital over labor.

The Economic Case for Free Migration

Rich Western social democracies place heavy restrictions on labor mobility. They make it tremendously difficult for unskilled laborers to move into their countries. They also impose heavy regulations on labor—such as licensing, minimum wage laws, and so on—which exclude very low-skilled laborers by rendering their work unprofitable. This is not a mere side effect of well-intended safety laws; often the real goal is excluding foreigners in favor of domestic workers.

The economic losses from immigration restrictions are staggering. By at least an order of magnitude, immigration restrictions are the single most inefficient and damaging thing governments do. The harms caused by the Iraq War or the mismanagement of the COVID-19 crisis pale in comparison to immigration restrictions.[4] Let's see why.

Among other things, closed borders are an import quota on labor. They function much like import quotas in cars, wheat, or other goods. Nearly all economists oppose import quotas—and

[4] See van der Vassen and Brennan (2018, chapter 11).

instead endorse free trade—because quotas lead to inefficiency and deadweight loss. They prevent mutually beneficial trades from occurring. They force people to buy from and invest in the less productive providers. They distort economies and concentrate benefits among the few at the expense of the many.

Figure III.1.1 illustrates the immediate effect of an import quota on a local market. The point where the supply and demand curves intersect—the equilibrium point—is what the price and quantity of the good or service in question would have been in the absence of protectionist restrictions. In a free and competitive market for labor, we would expect the market to approximate equilibrium.

At equilibrium, special things happen: First, all mutually beneficial trades take place, and so the quantity of labor supplied and the quantity of labor demanded are equal. Second, the gains to both consumers of labor (that is, the employers) and the suppliers of labor (that is, workers) are *maximized*. There are no further possible gains from trade.

The vertical line marked "quota" is placed at whatever quantity the government-mandated quota is, or, more realistically, at the resulting quantity that includes black-market imports. (In this case, "black market imports" means illegal immigrants.) The quota cuts off the supply of labor, stopping all trades to the right of the line from taking place. The triangle marked "W" represents all the lost income to workers, while the triangle marked "E" represents all the

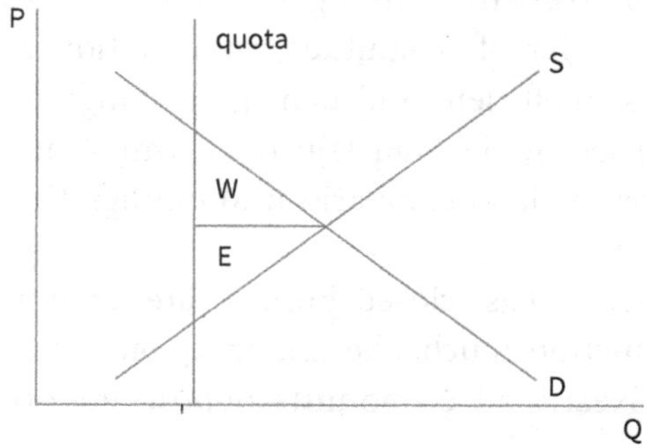

Figure III.1.1 Deadweight losses from import quotas on labor

lost income to employers. The immediate deadweight loss to the economy is W + E.

This model understates the problem. It ignores the costs to secondary consumers and others. It also ignores lost compounding growth year after year. It ignores the quality and enforcement problems arising from the black market that will emerge in the attempt to bypass restrictions. The total deadweight loss is higher than W + E.

Many economists have published peer-reviewed estimates of the deadweight losses from immigration restrictions, using the same well-established methods they use to calculate losses from other restrictions on international trade, by examining how existing internal and foreign immigration affects income, and so on. They generally estimate the deadweight loss of immigration restriction to be between 50% and 150% of current world product. The mean estimate in the literature is *100% of world product.*[5]

That is, immigration restrictions cut world production *in half.* Even the Great Depression did not cut world production in half. In 2017, gross world product (in purchasing price parity-adjusted US dollars) was about $128 trillion.[6] If people were free to work anywhere anyone offered them a job, world product might be around $256 trillion. We lose an entire earth's worth of production yearly because laborers are forbidden to move where their work is most valued and highly paid.

Now, some such estimates assume that workers will always move when this increases their net earnings. This assumption is unrealistic. People prefer to live near friends and family and want to avoid feeling "foreign." Still, economist Michael Clemens notes that even if we use more conservative estimates, based on empirical studies of worker's behavior, immigration restrictions still destroy on the order of $60 trillion, year after year.

The United States keeps detailed records on its legal migrants. This data allows economists to compare workers who have moved to

[5] Clemens (2011, 85).

[6] https://www.cia.gov/library/publications/the-world-factbook/geos/xx.html

the United States to their demographically identical, equally skilled counterparts who remained home. One major economic study examined the effects of immigration to the United States on workers from 42 poor countries. Workers' wages increased by factors of as low as 2.8 and as high as 15, with a median around 5. (The mean was higher than the median). That is, the median low-skilled worker from a poor country who moves to the United States sees her real, cost-of-living-adjusted income go up by a factor of about 5.[7]

If there were open borders, many low-skilled workers would move to the United States or other developed countries. These foreign workers would compete with each other, which would partly lower their expected per capita gains from immigration. However, by examining actual patterns of movement within free immigration zones, economists can nevertheless estimate the gains under open borders. Even then, the best estimate is that, under open borders, unskilled immigrants who move to developed countries would on average see their real (cost-of-living adjusted) income increase by least $10,000 USD/year.[8]

These figures *understate* the total welfare gains, because they examine only the direct and immediate effect on workers. Immigrants also remit money to family members in their home countries. Roughly 29% of Haiti's recent GDP comes from such remittances.[9] Economists Richard Adams and John Page discovered that every 10% increase in immigrants from a poor country to a rich country leads to roughly a 2% decrease in people living in extreme poverty back in the poor country of origin, for a resulting reduction in the poverty rate by about 3.5%.[10]

A large number of studies confirm these results; there is overwhelming evidence that remittances significantly reduce extreme poverty and enrich the people "left behind" in the immigrants'

[7] Clemens, Montenegro, and Pritchet (2009).
[8] Clemens, Montenegro, and Pritchet (2009).
[9] Desilver (2018).
[10] Adams and Page (2005).

countries of origin.[11] They benefit relatively poor and middle-income families in both urban and rural areas,[12] and lead to reductions in the number of people living on less than $1 a day and the poverty rate in poor countries.[13] Over time, the largest share of remittances is sent to poorer families, thus decreasing overall inequality.[14]

In one recent paper, economist Glen Weyl examines how differing immigration policies affect both total welfare and global income inequality. He notes that the Gulf Cooperation Countries admit a far higher number of immigrants on a per capita (and often absolute) basis than what he calls the "fortress welfare states" of the Organization for Economic Cooperation and Development (OECD) countries. Using this natural experiment, he then compares the effects of various policies: (A) Heavy in-country redistribution and provision of various public goods, (B) Monetary transfers from rich to poor countries, and (C) Open immigration.

Weyl finds that even at current levels of immigration, and despite the massive restrictions the fortress welfare states impose, immigration already accounts for a larger reduction in global income inequality and already produces higher welfare gains for the world's poor than all the redistribution *inside* or *between* countries. That is, right now, even with mostly closed borders, immigration is already doing more to reduce poverty and promote economic equality than internal welfare states or foreign aid. Further, when Weyl estimates what would happen if there were either much more redistribution or much more immigration, he again shows that immigration would do far more (in some countries, 10 times more) to increase the

[11] Among many other studies, see Acosta et al. (2008); Clemens and Bazzi (2008); de Haas (2005, 2006); Gupta, Pattillo, and Wagh (2009); López-Córdova, Tokman, and Verhoogen (2005); Pritchett (2006).

[12] Taylor (1999, 70).

[13] Richard Adams and John Page (2005) find that a 10% increase in a country's share of emigrants leading to a 2.1% decline of people living on less than $1 a day, and a 10% increase in remittances leading to a 3.5% decrease in the poverty rate.

[14] See Stark, Taylor, and Yitzhaki (1986); Koechlin and Leon (2007); McKenzie and Rapoport (2007).

welfare of the poor and reduce income inequality than either form of redistribution.[15]

As I said at the beginning of the chapter, markets want to be more egalitarian and to help the poor, but the social democrats won't let them.

The Intuitive Moral Case for Free Migration

There is also an independent moral argument for open borders. Consider this thought experiment from Michael Huemer:

> **Starvin' Marvin**
> Starvin' Marvin heads to the market looking for food. Marvin has little to trade. However, suppose there are people at the market willing to trade food for whatever Marvin has. Imagine that unless someone stops him, Marvin will successfully get to the market, make the trade, and eat. However, now imagine that you forcibly prevent Marvin from getting to the market. You post guards to keep him out. The guards continually capture Marvin and turn him away. Marvin can't barter for food. He starves and dies.[16]

In this situation, you do not simply fail to help Marvin. Rather, you violently interfere with Marvin and with the people in the market who want to trade with him. It wasn't your fault that Marvin was starving beforehand, but it's your fault he starves afterward.

Suppose we stipulate that Marvin isn't dying; he's just poor. Suppose that there are many people who want to trade with him on the market. His income would have increased by a factor of 10. When you interfere, he remains poor. Again, what you did is deeply wrong.

The way states treat most would-be immigrants seems analogous to how you treat Marvin in these thought experiments. Would-be immigrants want to take jobs elsewhere. There are people who want

[15] Weyl (2018).
[16] This paraphrases Huemer (2010).

to hire them, to rent or sell them homes, to sell them services, to befriend them, and so on.

But the state forbids all these trades and relationships. It had better have a damn good reason. Below, I'll examine some purported "damn good reasons" to block such trades. I'll argue they're not good reasons at all, let alone damn good ones.

Before we examine the counterarguments, notice again how national borders change how people think about the justice of interfering with people's freedom of movement. To illustrate, Fairfax County, Virginia, is one of the richest and highest achieving counties in the United States. It has low drug use, low crime, low teen pregnancy rates, very high income, very high employment, and very high educational attainment. Its government services and public schools are exceptional by American standards. Suppose Fairfax County announces it will forbid poor white people from West Virginia or poor black people from Washington, DC, to move in. Suppose the Fairfax's leaders offered the following justifications:

1. Poor people would overuse infrastructure.
2. They would swamp the county's welfare and social services.
3. They would reduce the quality of our schools.
4. They would undermine Northern Virginia's (NoVA) distinctively high-achieving, highly conscientious, professionally- and academically-minded culture.
5. They would depress local wages.
6. They could cause housing prices to skyrocket (because of sudden demand) or plummet (because people would flee to avoid living near the immigrant poor).
7. They would increase crime and reduce county health outcomes.
8. West Virginians and Washingtonians are not part of NoVA's social contract.
9. Our county is a democracy and we voted for these exclusions via a fair and democratic process.

You would be horrified if politicians said any of this. You'd say they are classist and racist. You'd probably make these complaints *even if* Fairfax officials could prove with fine statistical analysis and data that 1–9 are in fact true.

However, when the Prime Minister of Canada offers the same rationale for excluding Haitians, most people take these arguments seriously. Yet, it's not some unexplainable, basic moral fact that we have a right of freedom of movement inside a country but not between countries. There must be some real, identifiable feature that explains the difference, if there is one. Below, I'll examine (and rebut) some attempts to identify just such a feature.

Will Immigrants Depress Our Real Wages . . . Or Increase Them?

Many social democrats believe open borders would reduce the wages of domestic low-skilled workers. Are they correct? If they were, would protecting domestic wages justify immigration restrictions? I'll respond to the first question in this section and second question in the next.

The worry is reasonable. Politicians think that if you suddenly increase the domestic supply of unskilled labor, you'll thereby depress wages. In the same way, if we discovered mountains of gold, the price of gold would plummet.

Whether that reasoning is right, though, depends on whether foreign immigrants tend to be *substitutes* or *complements* for domestic workers. A *substitute* is a replacement for another good. For instance, Popeye's chicken sandwiches are a substitute for Chick-Fil-A sandwiches. If Popeye's cuts sandwich prices to $1, Chick-Fil-A will reduce its prices. If thousands of competitors to Chick-Fil-A appear, Chick-Fil-A's prices drop.

In contrast, a *complementary* good (or *complement*) enhances the value of other goods. For instance, a Popeye's chicken sandwich is a complement to Coke. You are willing to pay more for a Coke at Popeye's than you are at a convenience store. Similarly, you're willing to pay more for a combination of rum and Coke than you are for rum or Coke by themselves.

If immigrants are substitutes—if they will compete at lower cost for the *same* jobs as current domestic workers—they could indeed depress wages, at least to some degree in the short run. In the long run, the resulting productivity gains might still enhance everyone's income. But if they are complements—if they have different skills and would do *different* jobs—then will instead *increase* domestic workers' wages.

The extant economics research offers little support for the argument that we should protect domestic wages. Even if we assume, for the sake of argument, that immigrant workers are perfect substitutes for many domestic workers, economists nevertheless find that the negative effects on wages are small, temporary, and limited to a small subset of domestic workers. That is, while most workers see wages increase, some, typically the least educated, will see their wages decrease. Even these negative effects are temporary.[17]

When these pessimistic modeling assumptions are lifted—when economists try harder to determine whether immigrants are in fact substitutes or complements—the results are more positive still. Immigrants appear mostly to be complements rather than substitutes, and thus have a strong positive effect on domestic wages.[18] Immigrants are not the Captain Morgan to our Bacardi; they are the Coke to our rum.

The Priority of Conationals?

What if the research had found the opposite results? What if immigrants instead depressed most domestic wages over long term? Would that justify the fortress welfare states with their high immigration restrictions?

I am surprised that most social democrats say yes. Their supposed egalitarian and left-wing intuitions should nudge them the opposite

[17] Kerr and Kerr (2011, 12); Friedberg and Hunt (1995); Longhi, Nijkamp, and Poot (2005, 2006); Longhi et al. (2010); Okkerse (2008); Ottaviano and Peri (2008, 2012).
[18] Ottaviano and Peri (2008, 2012); Peri and Sparber (2009, 162).

way. Notice that hardly anyone would advocate restrictions on *internal* migration for these reasons. Imagine Virginia said, "Preserve high wages! No poor people from DC allowed!" Everyone would think this is unjustifiable. But when Canada says, "Preserve high wages! No Haitians allowed," they think it's reasonable. The "protect wages" argument doesn't itself explain why these two cases are different.

Let's examine what some social democrats have to say. Political theorist Michael Walzer says:

> The idea of distributive justice presupposes a bounded world within which distributions takes place: a group of people committed to dividing, exchanging, and sharing social goods, first of all among themselves. That world, as I have already argued, is the political community.[19]

Political theorist Stephen Macedo, following the philosopher John Rawls, says,

> if high levels of immigration have a detrimental impact on our least well-off citizens, that is reason to limit immigration, even if those who seek admission seem to be poorer that our own poor whose condition is worsened by their entry. Citizens have special obligations to one another: we have special reason to be concerned with the distribution of wealth and opportunities among citizens. The comparative standing of citizens matters in some ways that the comparative standing of citizens and non-citizens does not.[20]

Macedo agrees that this is counterintuitive. However, he argues that principles of distributive justice apply primarily *inside* borders rather than across them. He claims that people who live within the same democratic nation-state bear a special relationship to one another because they are coparticipants in collective self-governance.

[19] Walzer (1983, 37).
[20] Macedo (2007, 64).

Now, Macedo does not quite explain why being able to vote in the same elections gives rise to special obligations. I find the claim puzzling. I understand why I owe special obligations to my mom, my kids, or certain friends. I understand why I should prioritize their welfare over strangers'. But other Americans are *strangers* to me. I have no special connection to them. They vote in the same elections I do, they pay taxes to the same federal government, and they have the same passport designs. Some of them live closer to me than some foreigners. I don't understand why this means I should prioritize their welfare over Canadian or Haitian strangers. To me, that's as mysterious as saying I should prioritize the lives of fellow GEICO customers.

Macedo would probably claim that cocitizens are tightly engaged in some morally privileged web of cooperation, but that seems false. Whenever I do anything, I rely on the cooperation of millions of unseen strangers. In the modern complex economy, even something as simple as a #2 pencil is the product of the work of tens of millions of people. I work within a web of cooperation that stretches around the world. The American nation-state or my cocitizens are only sometimes overrepresented in that web.

On this point, Christopher Freiman offers a general challenge. Suppose you offer a substantive moral criterion that is supposed to explain why we should prioritize the welfare of conationals over foreigners. For instance, you might argue that conationals "speak our language," "are engaged in cooperation with us," "are less likely to commit crime," "pay taxes toward our common welfare," or whatnot. The problem is that for any plausible criterion you offer that is supposed to explain why I should prioritize an American's welfare, I can find millions of foreigners who better meet that criterion than other Americans. For any criterion you offer that is supposed to induce me to discount foreigners' welfare, I can find millions of Americans who meet that criterion more than various foreigners do. For instance, there are millions or billions of foreigners who contribute far more to my own welfare than most American citizens.[21]

[21] Freiman (2015).

Further, insofar as Americans are overrepresented in my web of cooperation, that's largely a product of the very immigration restrictions (plus tariffs and other trade restrictions) we're questioning. "You must prioritize your fellow citizens because you cooperate more with them than with others, and the reason you cooperate with them more is because we *force* you to do so" seems like a bad argument for immigration restrictions or for prioritizing their welfare over others'.

It's also puzzling why Macedo thinks "fellow Americans" is the special class to which I owe extra duties, rather than "fellow Northern Virginians" or some more narrow class. If sharing a government is what makes us owe each other more, then I should prioritize fellow citizens of my town over my state, and my state over the nation.

Suppose we grant Macedo that citizens owe each other more than they owe noncitizens. I can see how Macedo's line of argument could then justify denying immigrants access to the state's redistributive transfer payments. This would explain why my taxes fund welfare payments to relatively rich West Virginians rather than genuinely poor Tuvaluans.

But Macedo does not merely argue that Americans should pay higher welfare payments to other Americans. He must defend the claim that we may *actively harm* the world's poor and *actively interfere with their freedom* of movement in order to benefit "poor" Americans.

Even we grant that democratic nation-states should prioritize their own worst off, this doesn't license states to do whatever it takes to help them. We must still respect the moral standing of others. We must still comply with the rights others have against us. For instance, my special relationship with my kids explains why it's OK to buy them birthday presents rather than donate that money to poor Tuvaluans. But I may not actively harm Tuvaluan kids to help my kids. I may pay for lessons to help my kids compete for acting roles, but I may not hire a thug to beat up their competitors.

When rich countries restrict immigration, they do not simply prioritize their relatively rich domestic "poor" over the global poor when distributing resources. Rather, these restrictions actively and coercively interfere with others' liberty. They actively impose profound harm.

Do States Have the Right to Exclude?

Here are some other purported justifications for why states have the right to exclude immigrants:

1. States have the right of self-determination; the right to self-determination includes the right to determine who may enter and leave.
2. Just as clubs—the Shriners, a chess club, a softball league—have the right to determine which people may become members or not, so nations have the right to determine which people may become residents or not. People's right to association includes a right to choose not to associate with others.
3. The state owns—or perhaps all the citizens of the country collectively own—the country's territory as property. For that reason, just as you are free to forbid Haitian immigrants from camping on your lawn, so the state is free to forbid Haitian immigrants from renting a house or taking a job inside the country's territory. Or, just as a shopping mall is free to exclude potential customers, so the state may exclude foreigners.

If this book focused entirely on immigration, I would examine multiple versions of each argument at length. But for reasons of space, I'll offer quick criticisms of each argument.

Regarding 1: A state's right to self-determination is not a right to do whatever it pleases. States cannot, say, appeal to self-determination to justify mass censorship, outlawing disfavored religions, or imposing Jim Crow-style laws. Instead, the right of self-determination means that states have rights to make certain decisions within the scope of their legitimate authority. Whether the right to exclude immigrants falls within that scope is precisely the thing we're debating. Appealing to self-determination here begs the question.

Regarding 2: Suppose you and your friends want to form a chess club. You hold meetings in your privately owned estate. You vote and pass "By-Law 58," which forbids Chinese immigrants from joining your club. I admit, here, that your right of free association includes the right to form a racist chess club. The personal right of free association allows you to refuse to befriend black people, to avoid Mexican restaurants, or to attend race-based churches. I agree that right to freedom of association gives individual people tremendous leeway to refuse to interact with others, including for immoral or racist reasons.

Nevertheless, states are not analogous to clubs. Clubs are voluntary associations consciously formed by members for a given purpose; membership is determined by consent. The Chinese Exclusion Chess Club may not make me a member simply because my mom was, or because I was born near its clubhouse. It may not collect dues from me against my will.

States are largely involuntary organizations. The vast majority of people under the state's control do not and cannot consent to their "membership" in a state. Further, thanks to the very immigration restrictions we're discussing, people don't even have permission to "quit" the state the way you could quit the Chinese Exclusion Chess Club.

When the US government forbids me from hiring a Haitian or letting a Chinese immigrant rent my house, this is not like the local tennis club restricting membership to people in the neighborhood. The tennis club owns its grounds and sets membership rules. I consented to become a member, and I can leave any time. Rather, the US government is thereby restricting *my* freedom of association. It is stopping me from interacting with whom I please.

A closer analogy would be if the Chinese Exclusion Chess Club not only forbade Chinese members for its own club, but somehow used threats of violence to stop any other chess club from having Chinese members, and further, used its power to force everyone born nearby to be a member regardless of their consent. That's wrong.

Regarding 3: I'm skeptical that the way states control their territory is analogous to the way a homeowner controls her land. For one, the thesis that the state "owns" everything in its territory conflicts with the thesis that individuals and others inside the state own anything. If We the People of the United States collectively own all the property in the United States, then we as individuals do not really own any individual chattel, real estate, or businesses.

Further, if state's rights over their territory were analogous to property rights, that would prove too much. It would imply horribly illiberal conclusions.

Consider how property rights in my home allow me to do illiberal things. I am free to exclude Mormons from my house, and forbid all pro-Mormon speech, simply because it's my house. But the US government is not analogously free to exclude Mormons from the United States or forbid pro-Mormon speech because it's the United States' land. I am free to forbid any one from playing Taylor Swift in my house. But the US government is not free to forbid people from playing Taylor Swift music. And so on.

These three arguments fail. Still, suppose for the sake of argument, that states have the right to exclude any foreigners for whatever reason they please. Even if so, I could respond, "Sure, governments have the *right* to make that choice, but it's a terribly immoral and destructive choice—deeply harmful to their citizens and to the rest of the world." I could just grant for the sake of argument that states have the right to exclude foreigners, but then my point remains that it's terrible. Even if the state has the right to do it, it should not.

Can We Have Social Democracy *and* Open Borders?

Many people think open borders would bankrupt the expansive "fortress welfare states" definitive of modern social democracy. I'm not sure. After all, open borders would likely cause tremendous economic growth. A larger and more productive economy could sustain a larger welfare state. Perhaps it could then give more of that welfare to recent immigrants. If we make more pie, there's more pie to redistribute.[22] Readers should note that these tentative concessions help Arneson's side.

Still, there is some conflict here. The question is how much of a welfare state an open borders polity could sustain. Modern rich social democratic capitalist states, such as Norway, Canada, the Netherlands, and even the United States, have generous welfare policies. The people considered "poor" in these rich countries enjoy pre-tax-and-transfer incomes that are much higher than the world mean or median incomes.

Nevertheless, though their "poor" citizens are very rich by world standards, social democracies issue their "poor" generous packages of welfare benefits, including subsidized medical care, education benefits, training, unemployment insurance, pensions, food stamps, housing subsidies, and the like. Sweden, Norway, or the United States probably cannot afford to pay equivalent benefits to a sudden and large influx of genuinely poor immigrants, immigrants who fall far below what these countries consider their poverty lines. If not, is that a good reason to cut off immigration?

Relatedly, some economists, political scientists, and philosophers believe that increased immigration leads citizens to distrust each other, which in turn reduces their support for a robust welfare state. The idea here is that people tend to support government social insurance for people *like them*, but not for people they view as different. This is one unfortunate reason why welfare states seem to function better in more ethnically and religiously homogenous societies.[23] On this point, the social democratic philosopher David Miller says

> Redistributive welfare states rely upon trust among citizens that each will behave fairly under the terms of the scheme, paying taxes honestly and not drawing benefits to which they are not entitled. There is evidence, unfortunately, that as societies become more diverse, ethnically or culturally, levels of trust tend to decline; and this in turn makes it harder to win support for policies that may in practice benefit some

[22] See e.g., OEC (2013); Dustmann and Frattini (2013).
[23] Alesina, Glaeser, and Sacerdote (2001).

> groups more than others, even if this is not their intention. The upshot is that we may face a trade-off between higher levels of immigration and creating or maintaining a strong welfare state, assuming the latter is one of our goals. The evidence about this is not always easy to interpret.[24]

Even if so, there is a keyhole solution: Rich countries could admit immigrants, but deny them welfare benefits. We could build walls *around the welfare state* rather than walls around the country.[25]

That may seem callous, but it's far less callous—and less of a rights violation—than restricting immigration. If a country admits immigrants but denies them welfare benefits, it nevertheless greatly enhances their welfare. Regardless of whether a host country (A) admits immigrants without welfare benefits or (B) restricts immigration, it doesn't pay them welfare benefits. However, choice A greatly enhances everyone's welfare compared to B.

It's odd to think a spirit of equality or beneficence could justify anything different. Imagine saying to a potential Haitian immigrant to the United States: "We don't want you to be a second-class member of our society, so we'll forbid you from joining our society at all. Sure, if you came to the United States, your income would increase tenfold, and, hey, our income would increase as well. However, we can't afford or don't want to pay for your kids' schooling, so you'll just have to stay poor, and your kids will have to stay unschooled, in Haiti. Justice prevents us from treating you as a second-class citizen, so we'll treat you as a *non*-citizen, though that's worse for us both."

So far, we've discussed two options:

1. Exclude immigrants to protect the welfare state.
2. Admit immigrants but restrict their access to the welfare state.

From an egalitarian and humanitarian point of view, 2 is better than 1. But there's a third option:

[24] Miller (2018, 9).

[25] I got this phrasing from Nowrasteh and Cole (2013).

3. Admit immigrants but reduce the level of welfare services available to all, in order to give all residents equal access and benefits.

Which should we prefer?

Option 1 preserves the social democratic welfare state, but greatly harms the world's poor. Option 2 preserves the social democratic welfare state for the privileged and elite few but is better for (nearly) everyone than 1. Option 3 means the state would not offer a high level of cradle-to-grave welfare services to every resident but would instead offer relatively minimal welfare and social insurance services, equally available to all. Option 3 is the most *egalitarian* option. It avoids creating two classes of residents. Thus, I'd expect left-wing egalitarians to prefer 3 to 2. I'd expect communitarian nationalists to endorse 2 over 3.

Egalitarians would of course agree if we were discussing welfare policies inside single countries. Suppose we had definitive proof that Sweden could no longer afford to offer their generous social services to all citizens. Now, suppose we had two options:

A. Give the already richest 50% of Swedes access to ample welfare services, free schooling, and the like, but cut off the bottom 50% entirely.
B. Give all Swedes the equal access to means-tested welfare benefits but reduce benefits significantly.

I can't imagine any left-leaning person favoring A over B when it comes to domestic policy. For those same reasons, then, they should probably favor option 3 over 2 once we open borders.

Conclusion

This book debates which form of capitalism is best. My argument here is that from utilitarian, egalitarian, liberal/libertarian, and humanitarian points of view, open borders and open immigration are a

big win. Open borders could double world product, greatly enhance the living standards of the world's poor, and would improve the living standards of most people living in the richer first-world countries, too. Laissez-faire capitalist rules about immigration are far more conducive to ending poverty than implementing or maintaining social democracy.

We might have to make a choice: Either have social democracy or open borders. Perhaps at most, in the short to medium run, the rich social democracies could have a sort of split system, with social democracy for the domestic rich and a more laissez-faire, less generous welfare state for the immigrating poor. I've argued that insofar as we have to choose between social democracy or open borders, open borders wins and wins easily. Social democracies may be effective ways to spread the wealth among the world's most privileged people, but they are a barrier to helping the genuinely poor.

2

Economic Growth Beats Redistribution

A social democrat might respond to the last chapter as follows: "Sure, when it comes to promoting equality and eradicating poverty, open border laissez-faire systems are far better than closed-border social democracies, but open borders are not a live option. First-world governments are not going to open borders any time soon. Thus, we should ask which form of *closed-borders capitalism* is best. I say it's Sweden or Finland rather than some more classical liberal or laissez faire form."

This response concedes my argument from Chapter 1, but then argues that certain forms of social democratic redistribution are the second-best option. After all, even I agree that the social democracies aren't going to open borders, though they easily could.

I'll argue here that these redistributive policies are not even the second- or third-best options. To solve the problem of world poverty, economic growth is far better than internal or international redistribution.

The Moral Necessity of World Economic Growth

Some countries are rich and others poor. Some people are rich and others poor. Many people conclude poverty is a misallocation problem, too much here and too little there. Consider this thought experiment:

Debating Capitalism. Richard J. Arneson and Jason Brennan, Oxford University Press.
 DOI: 10.1093/9780190076467.003.0011

Misallocated Pie

Great Grandma baked a pie, enough to give all 206 of her great-grandchildren a full slice. But thanks to her poor eyesight, she cut the pie unevenly. She gave 20 great-children giant slices, 60 of them medium slices, and the rest tiny slices, so little that they'll go hungry.

Misallocated Pie elicits egalitarian intuitions: We should redistribute pie. Once everyone gets an equal portion, everyone will have enough.

The world is not analogous to Misallocated Pie. The distribution of wealth and income around the world, or even inside a single country, is not much like a pie cut the wrong way. Singapore is rich and China isn't, but that's not because God, the World Spirit, or Mother Nature gave China a small slice and Singapore a big slice. (In terms of natural resources, it's quite the opposite.) Singapore is rich because it has good institutions, and China is poor because it has bad institutions. China is now getting richer because many of its institutions improved and partially liberalized after 1979.

Simple arithmetic reveals that reallocating existing world income cannot eliminate world poverty. In Misallocated Pie, when everyone gets an equal slice, everyone gets enough. In the real world, allocating equal slices means *no one* gets enough. We cannot end world poverty without significant widespread economic growth.

In 2019, purchasing price parity (PPP)-adjusted world product was about $128 trillion USD.[1] That's the total value of all goods, services, capital investment, capital development, NGO activity, government activity, and so on, produced in one year, adjusted to reflect differences in costs of living.

Imagine, unrealistically, that I wave a magic wand that converts all annual production into consumable income. Imagine the magic wand split the world income equally among all living people. Imagine there is no loss of production.

PPP-adjusted per capita world product is about $16,100. That's slightly higher than the American poverty line (for one adult living

[1] https://www.cia.gov/library/publications/the-world-factbook/geos/xx.html.

alone). It's approximately the same per capita income as Issaquena County, Mississippi, the poorest county in the contiguous United States that is not majority Native-American.[2] By contrast, the relatively poor Appalachian region of the United States has a per capita PPP-adjusted mean income of over $39,000.[3]

Waving the magic wand doesn't end poverty. Rather, equalizing income means everyone is what Americans and Europeans consider poor.

It gets worse. The magic wand thought experiment *overstates* the case for global redistribution and understates the case for growth. I asked you to imagine that all current production is converted to income and distributed equally. In reality, most production could not, even in principle, be converted to income and transferred or redistributed to workers. Gross Domestic Product (GDP) includes various kinds of capital investment, government spending, infrastructure development, and other kinds of output that cannot be made liquid and transferred. Maybe half of world product could, in principle, be redistributed.

It gets worse. By hypothesis, the magic wand converts all economic output into consumable income. By hypothesis, then, governments, universities, nonprofits, and for-profit corporations produce nothing and cannot exist. The thought experiment imagines that we maintain current world per capita income without any capital investment or reinvestment, without spending any money on capital goods, without investing in new energy sources, without investing in infrastructure and transportation, without fixing any roads, factories, or tractors, without putting oil in the cars, and so on. It's nonsense.

It gets worse. We're also imagining that when the magic wand is waved, people continue to work at the same rate and with the same productivity. We're imagining white-collar workers who used to work 70 hours a week for high salaries keep working as productively

[2] https://apps.bea.gov/scb/.

[3] https://www.arc.gov/research/MapsofAppalachia.asp?MAP_ID=144.

in exchange for tiny salaries of $16,000 (or, more realistically, $8,000). We're imagining teenagers at McDonald's put in 20 hours weekly rather than using their $16,000 (or $8,000) to party. Real people aren't like that.

Bernie Sanders once campaigned on the claim that everyone in the United States should make a minimum of $15/hr. That's what he considers a bare minimum living wage. $15/hr in the United States translates into $30,000 PPP-adjusted dollars per year for an adult working 2,000 hours. Without further growth, it is impossible for most people around the world to earn what social democrats consider a living wage and to achieve a good standard of living. Right now, perfect equality means everyone everywhere is poor.

The upshot is that if you care about ending poverty, growth takes priority over equality. While there might be justifiable redistribution in some cases, redistribution remains secondary. Political philosophers sometimes talk as if there is and always will be enough stuff for everybody, as if the only issue were how better to allocate that stuff. Not so. Not yet, at least.

The Moral Necessity of National Economic Growth

Similar objections apply to redistribution within individual countries. Imagine, again, I have a magic wand. This time, it converts all current production inside each country into income, and then provide each resident of that country with an equal share of their per capita national income. There is no redistribution *between* countries, only inside them.

In the United States, with per capita GDP of over $70,000, every family of four receives $280,000! This magic wand would indeed eliminate poverty and deliver everyone what we consider an upper-middle-class standard of living. Hooray!

But, again, these numbers provide only an unrealistic upper bound on what redistribution could achieve. Remember, not all, and not even most, productive economic activity could in principle be converted to consumable income. We're imagining, for instance, that all the government spending on things other than employee and contractor salaries is converted to income. We're imagining there is zero capital investment, reinvestment, or maintenance. We're imagining stuff gets made without using any energy. We're imagining this $280,000 per family for four can be maintained indefinitely despite spending nothing on infrastructure or capital, despite not making any machines to make things, despite not sowing any fields, and despite not fixing any machinery that breaks. We're imagining everyone keeps working productively despite a guaranteed income of $70,000 per person, no matter what. All these suppositions are false.

Within poorer countries, it's more obvious that internal redistribution cannot solve the problem of poverty. My magic wand ensures every Haitian receives $3000 PPP-adjusted USD per year—less than 1/4th the US poverty line. Things are more equal, but everyone remains miserably poor. Haitians need growth, not equality.

Eliminating world poverty requires economic growth. Even in the richer countries, getting all citizens to the standard of living social democrats want requires significant and serious economic growth. Poverty cannot be solved by redistribution alone. When we see that GDP/capita in some rich country is $X, that doesn't tell us it's possible right now to use redistributive mechanisms to ensure everyone gets $X. It tells us instead that redistribution by itself—even with the help of magic wands—would at best give everyone significantly less than $X.

We need more pie, not mere rearrangements of existing pie. Above all, eliminating poverty requires creating the conditions in which more pie gets made.

Redistribution vs. Growth

We face a dilemma: Some things we might do to reduce the burdens of poverty today come at the expense of ending poverty tomorrow.

Current income depends on past capital accumulation, among other things. Our wages depend upon our productivity, and our productivity depends upon capital investment in the broad sense. People in rich countries earn as much as they do because of past investments in physical capital, human capital, research and development, and other productivity-enhancing factors. Once the right institutions are in place, countries with high investments in these kinds of capital grow rich. Those without, do not.

For this reason, we often must choose between helping some now and helping lots later. A dollar consumed is not a dollar saved and invested.

Suppose you have $100. Today you can feed 10 people with that $100. Suppose you instead invest that $100 for 50 years in an index fund with a real average rate of return of 7%, which is roughly the Dow Jones's rate of return (with dividends reinvested) between 1969 and 2019. Fifty years from now, that $100 becomes $3000 (adjusted for inflation). So, you can feed 10 homeless people today or 300 homeless people in the future. If you want to feed the hungry, it's not obvious which choice is better. (How much should we discount the welfare of future people?)

In fact, this argument understates the benefits of investing. The reason so few of us in rich countries need to be fed—why we're instead talking about redistributing to others—is because of past investments in productivity-enhancing capital. Investments today come at the expense of charity today, but also tend to make charity *less necessary* tomorrow. If we care about helping the poor, what ought we do? Should we feed people today or put people in a position tomorrow where rather than needing to be fed, they are instead pondering whether *they* should be feeding others?

Our world isn't static. Decisions about how to distribute resources affect what resources there are to distribute in the first place. Who gets what influences who produces what and how much they produce. Just as there's a trade-off between donating and investing, there's often a trade-off between redistribution and investing in growth. A dollar spent on welfare programs today could be used to ensure people don't need welfare programs tomorrow.

I don't want to overstate this. Some welfare programs and forms of redistribution (such as basic schooling) instead enhance growth; some do not. The exact relationship between redistributive welfare programs and long-term growth is hotly disputed among economists. Not all welfare programs are the same. Saying that the welfare state is good or bad, efficient or not, is too crude. Instead, one needs to look at individual programs. I'll review some of the empirical evidence below. There is very strong evidence that inter-state government-to-government transfers are largely ineffective (or worse), while intra-state transfers are more complicated.

Still, to illustrate the trade-offs in principle, consider an example. Suppose we compare two societies, Growthtopia and Fairnessland. Both contain three similarly sized economic classes. Both begin with an identical gross national income. Growthtopia chooses to prioritize economic growth over equalizing redistribution. Fairnessland chooses to prioritize equalizing income over growth. As a result, Growthtopia begins with a wealth distribution of 40, 15, 5 (from rich to poor), while Fairnessland begins with a distribution of 25, 20, 15. Growthtopia's per capita income grows at 4% per year; Fairnessland's grows at 2% a year.

World Bank economists David Dollar and Aart Kraay, after surveying 80 nations, found that on average when a country's real GDP grows at n% a year, the average income of the lowest quintile group and the per capita income grows at n% as well.[4] That is, they found that there is on average a 1:1 correspondence between growth in real GDP and the growth of the income of the poor. Additionally, this average is not a statistical artifact; most countries closely approximate the average. Thus, suppose each group in each country grows at the same rate as the country overall.

Now consider what happens to incomes over 100 years, as illustrated in Table III.2.1[5].

Eventually, the "poor" in Growthtopia become richer than the "poor" in Fairnessland. After 100 years, they are much richer.

[4] Dollar and Kraay (2002).
[5] For a similar chart, see Brennan (2007).

Table III.2.1 Income over time

	Growthtopia			Fairnessland		
	Rich	Middle	Poor	Rich	Middle	Poor
2000	40	15	5	25	20	15
2001	41.6	15.6	5.2	25.5	20.4	15.3
2005	48.7	18.2	6.1	27.6	22.1	16.6
2010	59.2	22.2	7.4	30.5	24.4	18.3
2025	106.6	40	13.3	41	32.8	24.6
2050	284.3	106.6	35.5	67.3	53.8	40.4
2100	2020.2	757.8	252.5	181.1	144.9	108.7

This illustrates the dilemma. In any given year, Growthtopia could better serve its "poor" by engaging in the kind of redistribution Fairnessland does. But doing so makes them worse off in the long run.

The hypothetical example above presumes there is a trade-off between growth and inequality. It presumes chasing growth means accepting greater inequality as a byproduct. In our world, that trade-off is not a given. Over the past two centuries, the world has become much richer. The increase in wealth was at first accompanied by an increase in global inequality. Over the past decades, however, the world's income distribution has changed dramatically. As poor countries, especially in Southeast Asia, caught up, global income inequality declined. In general, as countries grew richer, they first became more unequal, and then became more equal.[6]

In long run, slower growth is an invisible disaster. To illustrate, note that from 1870 to 2015, the average growth in GDP/person was 2.0% in the United States.[7] This is no mere average; the numbers year-to-year stick quite close to this average. 2% annual growth per capita is not much. Growth is difficult at the productivity frontier.

[6] Bourguignon and Morrisson (2002); Roser (2016).
[7] Jones (2016, 5).

Table III.2.2 Years needed for GDP/per capita to grow from $500 to $40,000

Growth Rate (%)	10	7	5	4	3	2	1	0.5
Years to $40,000/person	46	65	90	111	148	221	440	879

Suppose the United States had pursued economic policies that increased equality, but at the cost of reduced per capita growth. Let's imagine these policies cut average annual per capita growth from 2.0% to 1.5%. In that case, GDP/capita today in the United States would be about $25,000, about the same as Kazakhstan or Panama. Kazakhstan and Panama are richer than most other countries—but most Americans today are much richer than most people in either country.

Suppose instead redistributive policies cut growth down to 1% a year between 1870 and 2015. The United States today would have GDP/capita near $12,700 USD, the same as Egypt today, and roughly the equivalent of what we now consider the poverty line. Would you want to run your ideal welfare state programs with only the income and productivity of Egypt today?

Here's another way of looking at this issue. Suppose a country has a GDP/capita of $500. Table III.2.2 shows how many years it takes for that country to get up to $40,000 GDP/capita (on par with Western Europe) at different rates of growth.

There is ample debate among economists about the relationship between government redistribution and economic growth, or more broadly between the size of government and economic growth. In a review of the existing empirical literature, Andreas Bergh and Magnus Henrekson say that it's clear that "an increase in government size by 10 percentage points is associated with a 0.5% to 1% lower annual growth rate," though they say it's unclear whether this is *causal*.[8] In a more recent paper, however, they are more confident that it is causal.[9] Robert Barro argues that bigger governments lead

[8] Bergh and Henrekson (2011).
[9] Bergh and Herkekson (2016).

to less growth overall.[10] Jonathan Ostry, Andrew Berg, and Charles Tsangarides argue in contrast that redistribution can have a very slight positive effect on growth when economic inequality is very high.[11] Daron Acemoglu, James Robinson, and Thierry Verdier argue that some of the more generous social democracies may be free-riding on the innovations created in the more "cutthroat" capitalist countries; they enjoy growth by consuming and using the innovations created in the more cutthroat environments but then spend more cushioning their citizens against misfortune. However, if every country followed the same policies, this would lower overall growth.[12]

There is no consensus view on what the overall relationship is between inequality and growth, in part because what matters is not *inequality* per se but rather the mechanisms behind inequality.[13] Inequality caused by the deprivation of the poor hurts growth; inequality caused by the capital accumulation and savings by the rich enhances growth. Perhaps this is why some welfare states remain very rich while others languish.

Such concerns lead some social democratic philosophers to argue that principles of egalitarian distributive justice apply only after countries become rich enough. For instance, John Rawls argues that poorer societies should focus instead on growth and capital accumulation; they should worry about the distribution of income only when they have enough to go around.

Rawls was perhaps the most important social democratic philosopher of the past 100 years. Rawls did not see himself as defending the welfare state. Rather, he wanted to create a market-based economy in which the background rules regulating property, markets, schooling, and capital ensured everyone got enough without requiring continual government tinkering, adjustment, or redistribution.

One way to achieve that goal is to make a country very rich.

[10] Barro (1991).
[11] Ostry, Andrew, and Tsangarides (2014).
[12] Acemoglu, Robinson, and Verdier (2017).
[13] For a review, see: https://nintil.com/on-the-effects-of-inequality-on-economic-growth/?fbclid=IwAR3WA_34JWl4Prp52f4hFBXaZfcL4ItNqSR8Y83f920KxuLf2yrMDwED3Zc.

What Do We Mean by "Redistribution"?

As a conceptual matter, we should distinguish government-mandated social insurance schemes from government-mandated redistribution. Social democratic welfare states provide both, but the justifications for social insurance and redistribution are different.

Government-run social insurance is supposed to be more like a 401(k)/403(b) or private disability insurance, depending on the particular program in question. I pay into my 403(b) now and will collect the returns later. I have long-term disability insurance through my employer. I pay money now and hope *never* to collect benefits. However, the other customers and I voluntarily pool our risk together. We collect only if bad luck strikes. We're insuring against catastrophic loss. The lucky redistribute income to the unlucky, but people voluntarily participate because no one knows ahead of time who will be lucky and unlucky. Government-run "unemployment insurance" is roughly the same as my privately funded disability insurance program, except that I can't opt out of payments and the payout is poor.

Here's a rough way to distinguish social insurance from genuine redistribution: With government social insurance, you pay to participate. What you get depends on what you pay. The general expectation is that your taxes serve *you*.

With redistributive schemes, you receive some sort of welfare benefit in virtue of being needy, independently of what you contributed. Teen moms receive TANF payments and food stamps because they need them, not because they paid taxes toward them earlier, and not even with an expectation they'll "pay it back" later when they work full-time.

In practice, no bright line divides government social insurance and welfare/redistribution programs. Most social insurance programs involve some redistribution, and many redistribution programs have a social insurance element. Still, the philosophical and economic justification for social insurance and redistribution are quite different.

To argue for government-mandated social insurance, you'll usually want to show that there is some ubiquitous risk or danger. You'll then have to show that the market will not efficiently provide insurance against these risks, the way auto and disability insurance companies do. Perhaps there will be adverse selection, too few people will buy the right insurance, or too many people will be excluded for one reason or another. Then, you need to show the government has the right to force people to buy this insurance or participate in the scheme.

Even if you can prove that governments should force people to participate in an insurance scheme, it doesn't follow that the government itself must administer the service rather than merely require participation in private services. Automobile owners are required to purchase insurance but may choose among competing private firms. Instead of forcing people to participate in Social Security, with its impending budget problems and lousy rate of return, the United States could instead require citizens to invest 15% of their yearly income in private 401(k) plans.

The distinction between social insurance and redistribution matters for this debate. It's relatively easy to explain why social insurance programs involve conationals, but difficult to explain why government redistribution favors conationals over people in other countries. I will (maybe) receive American Social Security rather than a Swedish pension because I paid into the former but not the latter. Social insurance is primarily a mechanism by which the government forces you to protect yourself rather than forces you to help the less fortunate.

Yet when it comes to helping the less fortunate, the modern welfare states in Europe, North America, and elsewhere primarily redistribute income from their very rich citizens to their less rich citizens. In reality, their "poor" are rich compared to people in the rest of the world. An American at the poverty line is about ten times richer—an order of magnitude better off—than the average person in Haiti. If the point of the "welfare state" is to redistribute from the best off to the worst off, then modern social democracies are puzzling.

Instead of transferring money to their relatively rich "poor" citizens, shouldn't they instead send it to the genuinely poor outside their borders?

From a Moral Point of View, International Redistribution Beats Intra-National Redistribution

Philosopher Theron Plumer asks readers to imagine a thought experiment: Two people are drowning on your right and one on your left. You can push a raft to either side. Whichever side you choose, the other side will drown. Plumer says you should pick the two on the right over the one on the left. The numbers matter.

Let's extend this point. Suppose you have a spare sandwich. There's a starving person on your left. On the right, a college student says he hasn't eaten for an hour and would love a snack. You should give the sandwich to the starving person. The *amount* of good you do matters.

Imagine instead you find $100 billion. Suppose you can't keep it, invest it, or give it to someone you love. You must give it to the needy. As in the sandwich case, it seems callous to donate it to Americans at the "poverty line"—people, the top 15% or so of world income earners—*rather* than genuinely poor people elsewhere.

Just how rich are the "poor" in rich countries? Let's use the United States as an example.

In a rigorous paper examining American consumption over time, economist Bruce Sacerdote finds that Americans today enjoy a lot more *stuff* than they did in the past. Since 1960, American households *below* the median income—that is, in the bottom 50% of income—have gone from owning 0.5 to 1.5 cars on average. Only about 75% of bottom-income households had indoor plumbing in 1960; now they all do. The number of bedrooms and bathrooms per household has also gone up, even among the poorer households, and even though the number of people per household has gone down since 1960.[14] People have more space today than in the past.

As of 2005, 73.4% of Americans living at the official poverty line owned at least one car or truck, while 30.8% own two or more cars or trucks.[15] According to the US Census Bureau's Annual Housing Survey, as of 2017, basically all poor households (making $20,000 a year or less) have electricity, heat, a refrigerator, oven, microwave, and stove. About 90% of poor households have air conditioning in their home. Half have an electric dishwasher. Two-thirds have a washing machine and clothes dryer. If we confine our attention just to the very poorest households, those making less than $10,000, these numbers don't change.[16]

According to the US Energy Information Administration's Residential Energy Consumption Survey, as of 2015, nearly all poor households ($20,000 in market income or less) own LCD, plasma, LED, or projection TVs. Half have at least one smartphone. More than half own a computer.[17]

The US Census Bureau's Survey of Income and Program Participation examines patterns of food consumption and food deprivation. It finds that only about 6% of poor households report "sometimes" not having enough food, while about 1.5% report "often" not having enough food.[18] Amazingly, in 2009, during the Great Recession, it found fewer than 1 in 5 poor households, and only about 1 in 25 poor children, experienced even *one single instance* of reduced food intake over the past year due to a lack of

[14] Sacerdote (2020).

[15] U.S. Census Bureau, American Housing Survey for the United States, 2003 and 2005 Data Charts, at www.census.gov/hhes/www/housing/ahs/nationaldatahtml#jump2; U.S. Department of Energy, Energy Information Administration, *Housing Characteristics 2001*, at www.eia.doe.gov/emeu/recs/recs2001/detail_tables.html; U.S. Census Bureau, Survey of Income and Program Participation, 2001 Panel, Wave 8 Topic Module, 2003.

[16] Numbers derived from data at the US Census Bureau 2017 Annual Housing Survey, available at https://www.census.gov/programs-surveys/ahs/data/interactive/ahstablecreator.html.

[17] https://www.eia.gov/consumption/residential/data/2015/#electronics, Table HC4.5 Electronics in US homes by household income, 2015.

[18] US Census Bureau, Survey of Income and Program Participation, 2001 Panel, Wave 8 Topical Module, 2003.

money.[19] (However, keep in mind that some of this may be due to existing welfare-state or social insurance programs.)

Welfare-state redistribution is not social insurance; it's about transfers based on need. It's supposed to go from rich to poor. But as I keep saying, the "poor" in rich countries are relatively well off. If you have the kind of egalitarian or humanitarian intuitions that are supposed to underpin social democracy, you shouldn't at first favor social democracy with internal redistribution. You should favor international redistribution.

What the proponent of the modern social democratic welfare state needs, then, is some plausible moral principle that explains and justifies internal instead of international redistribution. But it's hard to find a plausible candidate principle that survives scrutiny. Consider each of the following candidate principles:

1. "We owe more to our fellow citizens!"
   Problem: This simply asserts the conclusion. *Why* do we owe more to our fellow citizens or conationals? We need a real principle.
2. "We have special obligations to our fellow citizens the same way siblings or friends owe each other more than they owe strangers."
   Problem: This argument reasons by analogy, but the analogy fails. For instance, suppose my relatively rich friend gets cancer and asks for help. Our friendship explains why I may, and perhaps even should, help him rather than help needier strangers. Fair enough.

But, to repeat the objection from the previous chapter, it's unclear whether conationals have any kind of special relationship analogous to spouses, siblings, friends, colleagues, or neighbors. They are literally strangers. We may have things in common, such as similar passports or paying taxes to the government, but it's unclear how

[19] Coleman-Jensen et al. (2011).

or why this could create the special obligations that arise in real relationships.

3. "We have special obligations to those within the same society, because we are involved in a web of cooperation from which we as individuals derive great benefit."

Here, the argument is that your own personal welfare depends in large part on your membership in and belonging to a particular society. You depend upon various background institutions, past rates of capital accumulation, and so on. In virtue of receiving such benefits, you owe more to fellow participants who helped create and sustain the social conditions that make you so well off.

However, there's no clear way in which the "society" in question here just so happens to be coextensive with the modern nation-state. Each of us is connected to billions of others in complex webs of cooperation, with some people close and others distant, with some strands thick and others thin, all organized by various overlapping formal and informal institutions, most of which regulate parts of the web but not the whole thing. Each of our webs is different and different parts of our individual webs are governed by different institutions. Your web does not match the borders of your nation-state, and indeed, your connection to and dependence on many people outside your borders is much stronger than for many people inside.

4. "We owe more to conationals because we have to justify the rules of the game to them. The institutions of our society won't be legitimate unless each member has a sufficient stake in those rules, and sufficiently benefits from them, that it's reasonable to demand they play along by those rules."

Left-liberal philosopher John Rawls made this kind of argument popular. But Rawls's argument faces the same problem as the last. There's no plausible interpretation of "society" that equates it with any modern nation-state. You are part of a web of cooperation, with different institutions regulating different parts of your web. Even the institutions that directly regulate you are not coextensive with your nation-state. They involve both more local and more international laws, rules, customs, and moral norms.

Rawls has no response to this objection, because he explicitly imagines away this complexity. In *A Theory of Justice*, for the ease of constructing his theory, he asks us to imagine an isolated autarkical nation-state, which people enter only by birth and leave only by death, in which all norms, customs, and laws are more or less uniform across the entire state. In Rawls's imaginary example, he stipulates that society is equivalent to all the members of a state, and we are all indeed subject to the same basic structure. But this has little to do with the real world. In the real world, nation-states do not have a uniform basic structure, and there is no "society" coextensive with the nation-state.

Even if you pretend that "society" is your nation-state and pretend that people within nation-states are subject to a uniform basic structure, Rawls's argument faces another problem. For Rawls, institutions are justifiable only if everyone subject to those institutions sufficiently benefits. But then, by Rawls's own reasoning, the very act of dividing the world into nation-states, with different laws and formal institutions in different places, and with membership almost always determined by accident of birth rather than by choice, has to be justified. Rawls argues that the fundamental rules must grant everyone equal liberties. Rawls argues that inequalities in income and other goods must be to the maximal advantage of the least advantaged. Rawls thinks luck should play little role in determining who gets what. What, then, about the inequalities that result from the bad luck of being born on the wrong side of a border? On Rawls's own reasoning, he should give priority to the welfare of the world's truly poor and should insist that the basic structure of the world be justifiable to all people everywhere. His theory should not be nationalist.

Further, even if we accept that we have special duties to compatriots, the amount of good we're doing still matters. The idea that we should prioritize our conationals does not mean that our conationals get strict lexical priority. Saving a foreigner from starving is still better than helping an American get a laptop.

There's one final moral reason why international beats internal redistribution: personal responsibility for poverty. Intellectuals with left-leaning intuitions often avoid asking to what degree individual people are to blame for their own poverty. But doing justice to our egalitarian and humanitarian intuitions *demands* that we ask.

The Brookings Institute—a moderately left-wing think tank—published a famous article showing that if poor American teenagers follow three simple rules, this more or less guarantees they will enter and remain in the middle class. The rules are: "finish high school, get a full-time job and wait until age 21 to get married and have children."[20] A person who follows these three rules, she has only a 2% chance of being poor as an adult, and a 75% chance of ending up in the middle class, defined here as making at least $55,000 a year. ($55,000 per year in the United States puts you in the global 1%.)

Note that these factors are causal, not mere correlations Having a child out of wedlock as a teenager, not finishing high school, and not working more or less guarantee you will be poor. In short, the study says the best way to avoid a black eye is to stop punching yourself in the face.

Perhaps because I grew up "poor" (by American standards, which means rich by world standards), I have far too much respect for the moral agency of the American "poor" to hold them to even lower standards than this. Saying to the American poor, "You can't really *help* but drop out of high school, have kids out of wedlock and as a teenager, and be unemployed," is in most cases classist (and often racist too). We disrespect them when we say, "Your situation is so bad you can't help but quit high school and have kids out of wedlock." The overwhelming majority of people can indeed help it.

When I make this argument, left-wing philosophers and legal theorists often balk. During presentations of this very argument at various universities, they will straight up say (I'm not kidding) that asking (most) poor American adults to use birth control, get a

[20] Haskins (2013).

GED, and take a job as a janitor is like asking a schizophrenic to stop hallucinating. These theorists says that the poor simply cannot help it. But when I ask these theorists if I can quote or cite them in print as examples of people who make this argument, they insist that I don't. Interesting.

Poor Haitians are poor because they live in Haiti. Haiti has dysfunctional institutions and little economic development. Almost everyone born there is doomed to poverty regardless of how conscientiously or prudently they live. In contrast, poor American, Swedish, Norwegian, or German adults are poor not because they were doomed to poverty by bad circumstances, but often because they make bad choices that cause them to be poor. Even those born by bad luck into poverty can escape poverty by making *easy* choices—such as not committing crime, not having children out of wedlock, and finishing high school. Once again, if I suddenly had $100 million or billion to donate to the poor, typical adult Americans at the poverty line are not the obvious choice. My left-wing intuitions direct my charity elsewhere.

But International Redistribution Doesn't Work Well

However, the moral case for favoring international redistribution over internal redistribution succeeds only if international redistribution works. Unfortunately, it does not work well. Note that this point helps Arneson rather than me.

Nobel-Laureate economist Angus Deaton notes that after World War II, hundreds of billions of dollars were spent on government-to-government and other forms of international aid. Between 2000 and 2010, governments provided $128 billion in foreign aid.[21] Looking at Africa over the past 50 years, Deaton notes inverse relationship between growth and aid:

[21] Coyne (2013, 47).

> Growth *decreased* steadily while aid *increased* steadily. When aid fell off, after the end of the Cold War, growth picked up; the end of the Cold War took away one of the main rationales for aid to Africa, and African growth rebounded . . . [A] more accurate punchline would be "the Cold War is over, and Africa won," because the West reduced aid.[22]

In a comprehensive review of the existing empirical literature, Hristos Doucouliagos and Martin Paldam conclude, "after 40 years of development aid, the evidence indicates that aid has not been effective."[23] In general, economists find that aid helps a bit in countries that have pretty good institutions, but tends to hurt in countries with bad institutions.[24]

Why would it *hurt*? Acemoglu and Robinson write,

> Despite this unflattering track record of "development aid", foreign aid is one of the most popular policies that Western governments, international organizations such as the United Nations, and NGOs of different ilk recommend as a way of combating poverty around the world. And of course, the cycle of the failure of foreign aid repeats itself over and over again. The idea that rich Western countries should provide large amounts of "development aid" in order to solve the problem of [world] poverty . . . is based on an incorrect understanding of what causes poverty. Countries such as Afghanistan are poor because of their extractive institutions—which result in a lack of property rights, law and order, or well-functioning legal systems and the stifling domination of national and, more often, local elites over political and economic life. The same institutional problems mean that foreign aid will be ineffective, as it will be plundered and is unlikely to be delivered where it is supposed to go. In the worst-case scenario, it will prop up the regimes that are the very root of the problems of those societies.[25]

[22] Deaton (2013, 285).
[23] Doucouliagos and Paldam (2006, 2009); Elbadawi (1999); R. Lensink and H. White (2001).
[24] Here, I draw from Coyne (2013, 51). See also Banerjee and Duflo (2011); Collier (2007); Easterly (2002, 2006); Moyo (2009); Hubbard and Duggan (2009).
[25] Acemoglu and Robinson (2013, 452–3).

The problem is that poor countries suffer negative feedback loops. They are governed by abusive elites, people who make a living (and stay in power) by extracting resources from their countries and people. In such conditions, to pour more money into a country usually means lining the pockets of the abusers, not feeding the hungry.

Foreign aid tends to make bad governments thrive without the support of their citizens, encourages factions within those countries (different agencies, bureaucracies, strongmen) to compete for power in order to gain control of the incoming aid, and tends to subsidize corruption. It escalates conflicts, civil wars, and human rights violations. Rather than inducing development and growth, aid often prolongs and worsens the conditions that produce poverty and need in the first place.

International aid and charity are often effective at producing predetermined outputs. If there is a famine, it's relatively easy to buy food and stop people from starving. But there is a distinction between *aid* and *development*. Development happens when a society begins to grow economically, and the institutional conditions that encourage growth. There is little track record of aid helping to spur economic development. The reasons why are clear: Countries need the right institutions to grow, but you can't export institutions the way you can send a sack of rice.

If these economists are correct, then this undermines the case for international redistribution. Rich countries are off the hook because their efforts fail for reasons beyond their control.

However, even this concession is too quick. After all, if Acemoglu and Robinson are correct, international aid fails because government-to-government transfers to reinforce bad institutions. But Sweden could instead transfer more money to relatively poorer countries with good institutions, if perhaps not the very poorest countries, which have bad institutions. Or Sweden could transfer more money to various NGOs that in turn directly serve the poor residents of poor countries, rather than looking for alternative forms of government-to-government aid.

Internal Redistribution Works, Sort Of

Note where we are in the dialectic: Open borders with its ensuing growth is best, widespread economic growth without open borders is second-best, international redistribution would be third-best if we can make it work, and social democratic internal redistribution is the fourth-best of the proposals we've considered.

Now we should ask—given all these concessions—whether internal distribution works, or whether it instead faces problems like those international redistribution faces. Estimating the effects of the welfare state is difficult in part because there are few natural or controlled experiments that allow us to disambiguate various causal factors. Here, I think, the evidence provides some support for social democracy. In the short run, at least, transfers make the relatively "poor" better off. In the long run, the results are less clear.

Even the Cato Institute—a libertarian think tank that's hardly a fan of the welfare state—seems to agree. Working for Cato, John Early, a former assistant commissioner for the Bureau of Labor Statistics, published a report examining the US poverty rate. He complained—correctly, as this is a matter of definition—that the US Census's official poverty rate does not take into account or include government transfers or welfare programs, including housing subsidies, the earned income tax credit, and so on, which the poor receive. Using the government's own data, he notes that once these transfers are included, the poverty rate in the United States drops from 12% to under 2%.[26] Early also notes that when social democrats complain about income inequality in the United States, they nearly always cite pre-tax-and-transfer numbers rather than the levels that obtain after income transfers. That might be fine as a way of illustrating the need to *continue* the programs, but it's misleading or dishonest as an argument for expanding them.

[26] Early (2018).

Or consider economist Rebecca Blank's book *It Takes a Nation*. She cites research comparing single-parent families in the United States and Canada. Both have similar rates of employment. During the time period she examines, a lower percentage of Canadian families lived at or beneath the equivalent of the American poverty line, because Canadian welfare benefits were higher.[27] In 1981, changes in Aid to Families with Dependent Children (AFDC) rules in the United States eliminated about 12% of recipients from eligibility. These were generally the best-off recipients, including especially parents who had jobs but still received AFDC. Various studies tracked what happened to the women who lost benefits. As Reagan expected, most mothers choose to work and earned higher private sector earnings. However, pace Reagan, the majority of these women had lower total income afterward.[28] In the short run, the amount they earned working was less than what they had received in welfare payments. (The study doesn't say what happened to these moms in the long run. Perhaps they stayed worse off. Perhaps their low-income jobs lead later to higher-income jobs.)

Blank claims that the disemployment effects of welfare benefits are not high. She claims that receiving $200 per month in AFDC benefits led recipients to work about 48 fewer hours per year.[29] Some recent research finds that more lenient welfare rules, which allow welfare recipients increased leeway to look for better jobs, lead recipients to receive higher overall long-term earnings and a higher chance of receiving employer-provided health insurance.[30] The idea is that giving welfare recipients more time to shop for jobs causes them to secure better jobs in the long run.

Sociologists Kathryn Edin, Laura Lein, and Christopher Jencks, in their book *Making Ends Meet*, defend similar results. They provide persuasive evidence that single mothers on welfare payments do better than single working moms. Mothers who leave or are kicked off welfare get jobs and make slightly more money overall, but must

[27] Blank (1998, 142).
[28] Blank (1998, 137).
[29] Blank (1998, 146).
[30] Lim, Coulton, and Lalich (2009).

pay for child care, transportation, and other costs. These increased costs consume their increased income. In the short run, they are better off caring for their kids themselves than working and paying someone else to watch their kids, and their kids are better off with maternal rather than daycare.[31]

However, these books do little to examine the long-term effects of employment versus welfare. Maybe the mothers who leave welfare for work are worse off at first, but in the long run they develop better résumés, get better jobs, and make far more money. On this point, in a recent paper, David Neumark, Brian Asquith, and Brittany Bass argue that "more generous welfare benefits lead to higher poverty and public assistance in the long run," and provide robust evidence that "more generous welfare benefits do not *reduce* poverty and reliance on public assistance in the longer-term."[32]

Social Democracies Primarily Provide Social Insurance, Not Redistribution

Regardless, most modern welfare states focus on providing social insurance rather than welfare-based redistribution. In most social democracies, the bulk of government transfers—when we include unemployment insurance, subsidies for schooling and higher education, tax subsidies, and so on—go to the middle class, the old, and the young, rather than the poor.[33] Government "welfare" spending mostly consists of medical insurance, social security for the very old, and education services for the very young, rather than redistribution to the poor.

The overall size of purely redistributive transfers in most modern social democracies is quite small. To illustrate, consider Table III.2.3

[31] Edin and Lein (1997).

[32] Neumark, Asquith, and Bass (2020).

[33] Using CBO data, Greg Mankiw reports on his economics blog that in 2011, the middle quintile of US households received $16,500 in transfers, while the bottom quintile received $9,100 and the second lowest received $15,700. See http://gregmankiw.blogspot.com/2014/12/who-pays-for-government.html.

Table III.2.3 Average income, means-tested transfers, and federal taxes per household, by income group, 1979 to 2016

Thousands of dollars					
	Lowest quintile	**Second quintile**	**Middle quintile**	**Fourth quintile**	**Highest quintile**
Income before transfers and taxes	21	45	72	110	291
Means-tested transfers	15	7	3	2	1
Federal taxes	<0.5	4	10	20	77
Income after transfers and taxes	35	48	66	92	215

Source: Congressional Budget Office 2016 Report. https://www.cbo.gov/publication/55413#data

below, which has recent data from the US Congressional Budget Office. Here, the CBO shows the amount of means-tested transfer that members of each quintile of income receive.

There were about 126 million households in the United States in 2016. Table III.2.3 thus implies that the lowest quintile received $378 billion in means-tested transfers, while the second lowest quintile received another $166 billion. Together, that's about 3% of US GDP in means-tested transfers to the poor.

Let's examine another rough estimate. The *social insurance* component of the US federal budget is gigantic: Medicare, Medicaid, and Social Security outlays were over $1.9 trillion in 2018.[34] The United States' social insurance programs are bigger than Canada's entire economy.

We can debate whether Medicare and Medicaid are redistributive or are social insurance programs. Medicare insures the old. Nearly everyone will eventually qualify for and consume it. The model is pay when you work, consume when you retire.

[34] https://www.cbo.gov/publication/55342.

Medicaid provides health coverage for low-income Americans, roughly 23% of the population.[35] It's more of a redistributive program, though rich contributors who experience bad luck might collect benefits.

The more obviously redistributive programs, such as SNAP (EBT cards, etc.), amount to less than $200 billion, depending on just what we count as redistribution versus social insurance. According to the Urban Institute, in 2016, state and local governments spent $638 billion on public welfare. This figure includes both social insurance and redistributive programs but does not include spending on education.[36]

All of these points together suggest that at most about 7% US GDP is transferred from richer citizens to the poor, if we include Medicare. The libertarian Cato Institute claims that total redistributive welfare spending in the United States is about $1 trillion, which amounts to about 4% of GDP.[37] I include their number here because, if they are biased, they would if anything be biased to exaggerate rather than downplay the size of the welfare state.

Similar remarks hold for other countries. The more left-leaning ones add a couple of percent in total transfers to their poor. However, the modern social democratic welfare states primarily provide *social insurance* and only secondarily engage in income-transfers or income-equalizing redistribution. Denmark and Sweden tax all of their citizens at very high rates—unlike in the United States, in which high-income families pay almost all the taxes and low-income families pay few taxes—but then provide ample tax-funded social services to pretty much everyone. What you get back is largely tied to what you pay in over your lifetime.

[35] http://econofact.org/evidence-on-the-value-of-medicaid.

[36] https://www.urban.org/policy-centers/cross-center-initiatives/state-and-local-finance-initiative/state-and-local-backgrounders/public-welfare-expenditures.

[37] https://www.cato.org/publications/policy-analysis/american-welfare-state-how-we-spend-nearly-$1-trillion-year-fighting-poverty-fail.

Conclusion

Social democracies may be the best places to live right now. The richest countries in the world tend also to be social democracies. (That does not mean they are rich *because* they are social democracies.) If you could choose to live anywhere today, you'd probably pick a liberal social democracy over any other state. So would I.

That should not blind us to how close-border welfare states hurt the world's poor and help perpetuate global poverty and inequality.

From a left-wing or egalitarian point of view, social democracy is overrated. It mostly provides social insurance to help the rich insulate themselves from some of the risks of markets. It "spreads the wealth" from the very rich to the merely rich, not to the poor.

If we want to help the poor, we would strongly favor open borders and rules that foster increased worldwide economic growth over the fortress welfare states. We would weakly favor international redistribution over the kind of internal redistribution we see (in surprisingly small amounts) in Sweden, Denmark, or the United States.

3
The Downsides of the Administrative State

Social democracies are not merely characterized by extensive tax- and debt-funded social insurance. They usually create extensive *administrative states*, which try to regulate, control, and manage the economy and other areas of life. Social democrats often argue that extensive regulation is necessary to ensure their economies function properly.

This chapter discusses some of the downsides of the administrative state. I won't argue for complete laissez-faire capitalism with zero government regulation. I suspect that there is an optimal level of regulation, but in general, most current social democracies have too much.

Why Liberals Should Be Suspicious of the Administrative State

Liberal political philosophies hold that liberty is the fundamental value that states must respect and protect. They hold that people have a right to live their lives as they see fit, as long as they do not interfere with others' equal rights. While all liberals agree that each person should have an extensive sphere of individual liberty, they dispute which liberties merit a high level of protection.

The administrative state directly interferes with individual liberties. To expand the scope of the state's administrative power generally means reducing the scope of individual citizens' economic

Debating Capitalism. Richard J. Arneson and Jason Brennan, Oxford University Press
 DOI: 10.1093/9780190076467.003.0012

liberty. By analogy, imagine the US government created the Sex and Love Administration (SLA), which regulated sex between adults the same way the FDA regulates food and drugs. Even if we could show the SLA made adults happier, safer, and healthier, most people would regard it as interfering with their liberty. To empower the SDA is to disempower individuals. Similar remarks apply to the state controlling economic or civil affairs. When we empower the administrative state, we generally take decision rights away from individuals and private groups and grant them to bureaucrats at regulatory agencies.

In contrast, the social insurance state does not, in itself, curtail most of our freedoms. When the government taxes away 33% of my income, I have less money. But if that is *all* it does, then I am still free to do as I please. On the other hand, if the government forbids me from opening a plumbing business, cutting down the tree in my backyard, buying marijuana, or whatnot, it immediately limits my freedom. It cuts branches off my tree of possibilities.

We could imagine a political-economic regime in which there is a completely or largely unregulated free market but in which the government taxes people to provide social insurance and some other welfare benefits. On its face, this regime seems much congenial to liberalism than, say, a low-tax regime that provides no welfare benefits, but which heavily regulates most enterprises, sets commodity prices, controls entry into markets, and imposes strict licensing rules.

This is not to say that administrative regulations are never justified. However, liberals of all stripes should by default be suspicious of the administrative state. It must be justified against the alternatives. Government regulation generally transfers decision rights from individuals to bureaucrats. The larger the administrative state, the more you have to ask permission to lead your life the way you want.

Democratic Control Does Not Empower Individuals

Some social democrats find this reasoning implausible. They claim that having extensive political control over the economy actually enhances freedom.

Now, we must be careful here. People often use the word "freedom" when they mean something else. Perhaps political control and regulation of the market economy sometimes make some products safer or make some things more predictable. Perhaps this justifies regulation, but we should not conflate safety and predictability with freedom. Or, perhaps some forms of regulation make market more competitive in the technical economic sense, by ensuring no firms have monopsonistic or monopolistic bargaining power. These kinds of regulations and interventions can, in principle, enhance individual freedom by stopping others from dominating markets. But this isn't the issue I have in mind here.

Instead, many social democrats believe democratic control of the economy enhances freedom simply because it is democratic. In their mind, to subject the economy to democratic control means giving every person a say over how the national economy goes. They might argue as follows:

> In an unregulated market economy, individuals are subject to market forces beyond their control. Indeed, the more competitive the market is, the less power anyone has. We are all pushed around by the forces of supply and demand. When we subject the market to democratic oversight, then we give ourselves a say over how the economy goes. Instead of being victims of impersonal forces, we appoint ourselves the masters of the economy. Now We the People decide what form our economy takes and which direction it goes.

In short, just as people think that replacing a monarchy with a democracy enhances freedom in virtue of giving citizens a say over government, they might think that replacing an unregulated market economy with a democratically regulated economy does the same.

Though I see people making this argument to defend government control of the economy, most would reject this reasoning if we applied it to other spheres of life. Suppose I said, "Both the marketplace of ideas and the market for love are unregulated, a Wild West, dog-eat-dog competitions, in which individuals are forced to compete for attention, acceptance, love, and so on, all while subject to forces over which they have no control and have no say. We should thus have the government extensively regulate religion, speech, sex, and dating, but then give each person an equal vote to appoint the legislators who will indirectly oversee the regulating bureaucrats." I suspect you would regard this proposal not as enhancing individual freedom, but instead restricting and transferring power away from individuals to government agents. You would say that even though it's probably true that the marketplace for ideas and for love is indeed subject to impersonal forces, is highly unfair, and faces extensive "market failures" such as unequal bargaining power, persistent irrationality among consumers and suppliers, and asymmetric information.

The argument that democracy inherently enhances personal freedom is also implausible because a vote is not a meaningful say. Casting a vote is like playing the lottery—there is some small chance that there will be a tie, and that your vote will decisively break that tie. Even if you miraculously broke a tie, and even if the election were not then decided in court by lawsuits, you would at best decide the election of one congressperson or a president, who in turn would have only limited control over what the bureaucracy does. To say that your vote gives you power over the world is like saying a bucket gives power over the ocean.

I make personal decisions over what to wear each day, what to eat, what color toothbrush to have, what to watch on television, over what to write about for my dissertation, where to go to college and graduate school, which job offers I would accept; about whom to marry, whether to have a child, what to choose for a career. The same goes for you. If all these choices had instead been subject to democratic decision-making, we'd regard that as taking the choice away from us and giving it to the democratic body. Even if we each had an equal vote in this body, it would mean a severe loss of autonomy for each of us.

Now, perhaps social democratic control of the market economy is justifiable for some other reason. But we shouldn't argue that it's in itself a way to enhance our freedom. Frankly, it's silly that so many activists and philosophers say otherwise. Instead, a good argument for economic regulation should include each of these elements:

- Markets have problem that are sufficiently severe that we should grant government the power to fix them.
- When we grant government that power, it will in fact fix the problem at a price worth paying.
- When we grant government that power, it won't thereby cause even worse problems.
- There is some principled reason why governments should have this regulatory power over the economy—and the power to restrict individual freedom—but not (on the same grounds that justify economic regulations) over other areas of life, such as religion, speech, friendship, love, voting, and so on, that suffer from similar problems. (Otherwise, the proponent of regulation must on pain of inconsistency extend their argument to these other areas of life.)

Sometimes advocates for regulation successfully discharge this burden of proof. But often their arguments are little better than this: "Government makes better economic decisions than the market. How do I know? I see what looks like a market failure to me and I imagine things going differently if government does something."[1]

Robert Nozick's General Challenge to Left-Liberals

Let's start by reflecting on the last bullet point. In part II of *Anarchy, State, Utopia*, Robert Nozick argues that a "more-than-minimal state" cannot be justified. The minimal state provides police and military protection, courts, and a modicum of public goods, and that's it.

One of Nozick's main moves is to point out that many arguments for the more-than-minimal state, if applied consistently, would not merely show that the state should regulate the economy. They would

[1] James Hanley offered this point on Facebook as a parody of how many arguments for public policy go.

also show that the state should curtail civil rights and regulate social life as well.

For instance, someone on the Left might say, "Asymmetric information in auto markets means that some people can exploit others, so the government ought to heavily regulate auto markets." A Nozickian response might be: "There's even more asymmetric information in dating markets, and the effects of bad relationships are even more devastating than paying too much for a used car. Shouldn't we thus heavily regulate dating in the same way?" A left-liberal would probably say that of course we shouldn't, but this tells us that the asymmetric information argument wasn't doing the real work for that left-liberal. The left-liberal instead has some other reason, hidden away, for treating the two differently. The left-liberal has already decided that the problem of asymmetric information is *not* grounds for government regulation in, say, dating, speech, or religion. Accordingly, we need to see what the left-liberal's actual hidden argument is.

Nozick notes that many claim that governments should regulate the economy and redistribute wealth in order to produce equal opportunity. Often, Nozick notes, this argument relies on the metaphor of society being a race. That metaphor is misleading. In a race, one person can win only if others lose. However, society is not a race. You getting richer doesn't automatically mean I get poorer. You succeeding in your job doesn't mean I fail in mine. It's not as though there is one person handing out prizes and positions. It's not as though we are all racing along one track with one prize at the end. Rather, there are millions of people choosing each day to interact with millions of others. The race metaphor is bad. If society were a zero-sum race, society wouldn't be a game worth playing.

Nozick adds that arguments like this have implications that the people making those arguments are not prepared to endorse. People say that in the market, the winners should compensate the losers, or the government should intervene to reduce or eliminate unequal outcomes. But then Nozick asks, if so, why not say the same thing about, say, the dating market?

Nozick asks us to imagine that other men desperately wanted to marry his wife, but she turned down because they were dumber and uglier than Nozick.[2] Nozick asks, should he or society compensate those suitors for their loss? Should they pay for the suitors' plastic surgery, or for classes to improve their intelligence? Should we consider handicapping smart, good-looking men in order to prevent them from having unfair and unearned advantages in the dating market?

Lest that seem like a silly thought experiment, note that some empirical work claims that the dating market is in fact extremely unequal. For instance, on Tinder, some people do much better than others. Among heterosexuals, the bottom 80% of men are competing for the bottom 22% of women, while the top 78% of women are competing for the top 20% of men. (Here, "top" and "bottom" means as measured by interest from others.) If we portray the distribution of "swipes right" like the distribution of income, then heterosexual women compete in a market with a GINI-coefficient of 0.324, while straight men face a market with a GINI-coefficient of 0.542. That means the dating market for men (on Tinder, at least) is as unequal as the most unequal countries in the world.[3] If, as most people say, love and sexual companionship are far more central to the good life than money, why not conclude that the government should intervene to reduce sexual and dating inequality?

Again, most would not bite that bullet. But again that means that "reducing inequality" or "compensating the losers" are not doing the real work in their arguments for economic regulation.

Nozick makes a similar move against other arguments for intervention and regulation. For instance, some people claim that the government should regulate the economy because people have a right to a say over what important decisions that affect their lives.[4] But, Nozick notes again, at least at first glance, this argument applies

[2] Nozick (1974, 237–8).
[3] https://quillette.com/2019/03/12/attraction-inequality-and-the-dating-economy/.
[4] Nozick (1974, 268–71).

equally well for allowing the state to submit personal decisions to democratic control. He asks us to imagine a woman has four suitors. We would never think that these five people, or their friends and family, should get to vote on her decision, even though they "should have a right to say in important decisions that affect their lives." Similarly, suppose you get a job offer in another city. Suppose you leaving your job hurts your current coworkers more than it helps you. We wouldn't think this means your coworkers have the right to vote on whether you may leave. Or, suppose your life will go well only if at least 20 million people accept your religion. We wouldn't think this gives you a right to vote on which religion others may follow.[5] And so on.

Nozick expects that the left-liberals against whom he argues would consider such suggestions absurd.[6] He agrees. His point is that they should abandon their arguments for equality of opportunity in other contexts as well, unless they can somehow identify a principled reason why these arguments apply only to economic cases and not others.

If you don't like Nozick's specific examples, come up with your own. Consider the kinds of reasons people offer for government regulation of the economy, including the misallocation of resources, asymmetric information, persistent consumer or supplier irrationality and bias, systematic risks, or systematic externalities. With a little effort, you can see these same problems occurring in personal and religious speech, in how people date or find friends, in how they form associations, in their choice of religions, in their choice of what to study in college, or in their political speech and behavior. If these are grounds for government regulation of the market, they are at first glance equally strong (and often stronger) grounds for regulating people's religious, political, romantic, or civic behavior. But most people treat the two differently.

[5] Nozick (1974, 268–71).

[6] For what it's worth, I know of one far left philosopher who bites the bullet and says that the winners of competition for love should compensate the losers.

We need a principled reason why the government should *not* regulate and constrain our personal lives but *may* regulate our economic decision. Usually, no such argument is forthcoming other than a brute, table-pounding insistence that obviously personal liberties are different.[7] In some cases, philosophers have attempted to defend the claim that the two are different, but it's unclear whether their arguments work.[8]

Taking Government Failure Seriously, Seriously

Political scientist Michael Munger asks us to imagine that the State Fair decides to hold a "Big Pretty Pig" contest. Suppose there are only two entries. The judge takes a long look at the first pig and exclaims, "My God, that's one ugly pig! You know what, let's just give the prize to the second one." The problem is that the unseen second pig might be even uglier.

It's an obvious mistake, but many social democratic economists, political scientists, and philosophers make this same mistake when they judge market institutions. They complain about how ugly some institutions are in practice, and then say we should go with their favored alternatives instead. But they fail to examine whether their favored alternatives are even uglier. So, for instance, they might identify a market failure and propose that we empower government to solve the problem, but fail to consider whether government failure in this area might be even worse than the market failure, or whether empowering the government to correct various market failures might lead to systematic downsides.

Markets can fail. So can governments. I think once we account for both market *and* government failures, this heavily favors markets over governments. As the Nobel laureate libertarian economist Gary

[7] Murphy and Nagel (2002, 65) responds to an objection like this by simply asserting that civil liberties are at the core of the self but economic liberties are not. Rawls, to his credit, tries to offer a principled reason for treating them differently, but he never completes his argument, and his reasoning runs into serious problems. See Brennan (2020).

[8] Brennan (2020).

Becker says, "on the whole, government failure is far more pervasive, damaging, and less self-correcting, than is market failure."[9] He thus recommends government intervention only in cases where market failures are serious and persistent. The general presumption should be in favor of markets.

The typical undergraduate microeconomics textbook describes cases where markets are unlikely to produce efficient outcomes. These textbooks often claim that, in principle, government intervention could solve the market failure.

However, these textbooks tend to assume that government both (1) has full information about how to solve the problem, (2) has both the good faith and competence to use its power to solve the problem, and (3) that the government fixing the problem will do more good than harm. When textbooks say governments can fix market failures, it's as if they said *omniscient angels can intervene to solve market failures*. Thus, when undergraduate textbooks recommend government intervention, they often mean intervention by *idealized* government, not necessarily by real governments. In the real world, sometimes the best response to serious market failure is to suck it up and live with it. Let's consider some kinds of government failure.

1. Governments can fail through *over*regulation. Some regulations have no real benefit—they just waste money and make innovation harder. Other regulations save lives, but at too high a cost.

In a famous study, Tammy Tengs and her colleagues (none of whom are libertarian, for what that's worth) measured the cost-effectiveness of 587 regulations. They found great variation. The Federal Aviation Administration's regulations cost, on average, $23,000 to extend one person's life one year. The Environmental Protection Agency's regulations average $7.6 million per life-year extended.

The costs of overregulation are usually hidden. Suppose we insist that drugs are proven perfectly safe and effective before we allow

[9] https://www.becker-posner-blog.com/2011/09/market-failure-compared-to-government-failure-becker.html.

them on the market. Regulating medicine causes *drug lag* and *drug loss*. "Drug lag" refers to the time needed to get a drug approved. In the United States, average drug lag is over 12 years. In that time, people suffer or die from whatever the drugs would cure. "Drug loss" refers to how regulations prevent useful drugs from being developed or coming to the market. It costs over $1 billion on average in the United States to bring a drug to market. This means that drug companies will only pursue highly profitable drugs with wide appeal (such as drugs for erectile dysfunction) rather than less profitable drugs with narrow appeal. It also means drug companies will not make drugs that only help the poor.

Overregulation can also be a *systematic* problem. Any given regulation, in isolation, might be justified. But the cumulative effect of these regulations, even if they are each justifiable in isolation, might be terrible. On this point, in a recent paper, economists John Dawson and John Seater examine how US federal regulations affect economic growth. They find that these regulations cut growth but about 2% a year. Over a 55-year period, the cumulative effect is devastating: If the US economy had stayed as regulated as it was in 1949, instead of adding extensive regulations annual, US GDP in 2005 would have been about $54 trillion instead of a mere $13 trillion, meaning that there was cumulative deadweight loss of $38 trillion a year.

Other studies find similar results. For instance, a 2005 World Bank study claims that a 10-percentage point increase in regulation reduces GDP-per-capita growth by half a percentage point.[10]

These numbers may seem fantastic, but they are not. Remember, as we discussed in the last chapter, in a given year, a little less growth seems like no big deal at first. But compound that year after year, and it means the difference between a country being rich or poor. US GDP/capita would have been three times what it is today if only the government had had a lighter touch. Suppose Dawson and Seater are wrong, and the loss is *only* 1% a year. Over 55 years, that's a huge loss. If your $100 grows at 3.5% a year, you'll have $664 in 55 years. At 2.5% growth per year, you'll end up with only $389. At 1.5%, you'll

[10] Loayza, Oviedo, and Serven (2005).

end up with only $227. Regulation can do quite a bit of visible good, but it also imposes a great deal of invisible harm. To pay for itself, it all needs to be worth the forgone growth.

The reasons for slower growth are myriad: Regulations drive up the cost of doing business, discourage investment, discourage entrepreneurship, and function like a tacit tax that eats away at capital growth.[11]

Note that in many cases, regulations also systematically drive up prices. As an example, consider the housing market in California. California's regulators (at both the state and local levels) make it difficult to obtain permits to build new housing. They also impose a wide range of regulations that make building those new homes more expensive. In a recent paper, economists John Quigley and Steven Raphael carefully measure how housing regulations affect California's home prices. The results are startling: *each* major regulation passed between 1990 and 2000 leads to home prices increasing between 3.0% and 4.5%, and rental prices increasing between 1.0% and 2.3%.[12] Housing is expensive in California, not because we've run out of space or because labor costs are higher today. It's expensive because restrictive codes mean hardly any new homes get built—causing a massive shortage and driving up prices—and restrictive regulations make housing more expensive than people can afford.

In a recent study, economist Diana Thomas considers how regulations protect against both large and small risks. There is a good case, she thinks, for eliminating large risks. However, she claims, more affluent voters tend to demand that the government insulate us from small risks as well. The problem, she says, is that compliance with regulations drives up the costs of goods, including food, housing, clothing, and the like. Affluent citizens spend a smaller percentage of their income on such goods and can easily afford them; to them, increased regulation seems like a good deal. Poorer citizens spend a much higher percentage of their income on these goods and have difficulty affording them. She concludes that poor households

[11] Dawson and Seater (2013).
[12] Quigley and Raphael (2005).

spend between six and eight *times* the share of their income on regulatory compliance costs compared to affluent households. Regulation functions, in effect, as a regressive task that disproportionately harms the poor.[13]

Economists Dustin Chambers, Patrick McLaughlin, and Laura Stanley find a related result. They use the Federal Regulation and State Enterprise Index, which measures and weighs the differing levels of regulation different US states face. After all, some states, such as California, are far more regulated than others, such as Virginia. Further, due to differences in industry, some face a higher effective federal regulatory burden than others. They find that a "10 percent increase in the effective federal regulatory burden on a state is associated with an approximate 2.5 percent increase in the poverty rate."[14] There is good reason to think the relationship is causal rather than a mere correlation, because the costs of regulation are disproportionately felt by the poor.

The progressive left often complains that corporations are too big. However, their favorite regulations tend to distort the market in favor of larger and larger corporations. The more we regulate the economy, the bigger Big Business tends to be. The reason, again, is that complying with regulations costs money and time. The larger your company is, the more easily you can keep up with the rules. The US Small Business Administration (SBA)—a government agency—reports that complying with all regulations costs firms on average $10,585. However, these costs are not evenly dispersed. The SBA claims that small businesses face about 36% higher costs per worker than large businesses. Some of its earlier studies had estimated that small firms pay 60% more costs per worker than large firms to comply with federal regulations.[15]

2. Governments can fail by *mis*regulating. Sometimes governments just make bad choices.

[13] Thomas (2019).
[14] Chambers et al. (2019).
[15] https://www.researchgate.net/publication/286350317_The_Impact_of_Regulatory_Costs_on_Small_Firms.

Take the issue of housing prices, again. Tokyo has a very high population density of nearly 6200 people per square kilometer.[16] Los Angeles is less than half that: 2910 per square kilometer. Nevertheless, housing is overall about twice as expensive in Los Angeles, though the price per square foot is slightly higher in Tokyo.[17] (Los Angeles' apartments and houses tend to be bigger.) What's of more interest here are the trends. Housing prices in Los Angeles generally increase by multiple percentage points year after year, while housing prices in Tokyo have remained relatively flat. It's worse elsewhere. Housing prices increased over 400% between 1995 and 2015 in London, and over 200% in that period in San Francisco. In Japan, overall, they stayed the same.[18] What's the difference?

Economists think it has to do with regulation, in particular, with badly designed zoning regulations in the United States and especially in California. In California, city central planners will insist that only certain forms of construction can occur in a given area. This spot must have single-family homes. This spot should have retail. This spot may have apartments. Japan, in contrast, has a far more laissez-faire approach. They impose a maximum "nuisance level" in a given zone, but otherwise allow for significantly mixed zoning. Housing can be right next to light industry and retail. The result: Though Japan has half the population of the United States, it is building the same number of housing units per year. Housing is cheaper in Japan because there's more of it, and the reason there's more of it is that it's much easier to build it. The reason it's easier to build it is that regulators get out of the way.[19]

Note that Japan did have a housing bubble in the late 1980s. When the bubble burst, lawmakers correctly diagnosed that overregulation—which drove up housing prices, which in turn incentivized speculation in housing—was to blame. They responded

[16] http://www.metro.tokyo.jp/ENGLISH/ABOUT/HISTORY/history03.htm.

[17] https://www.numbeo.com/cost-of-living/compare_cities.jsp?country1=United+States&city1=Los+Angeles%2C+CA&country2=Japan&city2=Tokyo.

[18] http://www.ft.com/cms/s/0/023562e2-54a6-11e6-befd-2fc0c26b3c60.html?siteedition=intl.

[19] https://www.wsj.com/articles/what-housing-crisis-in-japan-home-prices-stay-flat-11554210002.

by deregulating zoning and housing construction. Now while the poor struggle to afford housing in California, New York, and London, the poor can more easily afford housing in Japan.

Consider another example. Despite what historians say, in the late 1800s, there was no unregulated free market in banking. Instead, banks were also regulated in ways that forced them to accept undue risk. In particular, thanks to the 1927 McFadden Act, they were forbidden from forming branches and thus using one market to ensure another. They were instead required to serve—and thus have all their risk tied up in—a single area. During the Great Depression, the United States had about 9,000 bank failures, despite having a central bank. Canada, in contrast, allowed banks to have branches across provinces and thus allowed them to spread their risk. It had no central bank and yet had zero bank failures in the same period.[20]

Consider another example. Automobiles have safety ratings, often expressed in terms of stars. Rich people like me often drive 5-star autos. I can afford to pay top dollar. But in India, until recently, there were a wide range of zero-star cars on the market. These cars are indeed very unsafe. India has now committed to banning such unsafe cars and will push to have highly stringent regulations. That sounds great, but it may turn out to be a safety disaster. The reason is that only about 6% of Indian households own cars. About half instead own motorcycles. The zero-star cars were competing more with motorcycles than with other cars. When the new safety regulations come in, they will drive up the price of cars. (An airbag costs at least $250, which is about 1/20th the average yearly income in India.) Thus, the regulations might simply push people to drive motorcycles instead, which are far less safe than zero-star cars.[21] For a domestic analogy, consider how the US government reacted to learning that some high school kids were dying after purchasing contraband, THC-infused vaping cartridges on the black market. This may reduce teen vaping and save some lives, but it might

[20] https://www.aei.org/carpe-diem/great-depressionnot-a-single-canadian-bank-failed/.
[21] https://marginalrevolution.com/marginalrevolution/2016/05/safety-is-relative.html.

also induce teenagers to switch to cigarettes, which are far more dangerous.

3. Governments can fail by enabling *rent seeking*. "Rent seeking" is a fancy word for cronyism and pork barrel politics. An individual, firm, or union engages in rent seeking when it tries to change the laws or regulations, or how the laws and regulation are administered, in order to secure a special benefit for itself at the expense of others. Rent seekers try to get the government to manipulate the market in their favor.

Making money in a free market is hard. You have to be better than your competitors. Making money by rigging the rules is easier. You just need to have better connections. When well-meaning voters and politicians create government power in order to control and restrain corporations, corporations often capture this very power. When we attempt to control corporate power through government, we often instead end up *giving* corporations even more power.

Firms sometimes lobby the government to impose certain regulations or taxes on their industry, because they expect these regulations or taxes will harm the firm's competitors more. (For instance, Amazon wants an Internet sales tax in order to hurt eBay.) Or, a firm might lobby for a subsidy, tariff, or trade barrier. Subsidies lower the firm's costs, while tariffs and trade barriers reduce competition. Or, a firm might try to socialize its risks, such as when a bank induces a government to bail out bad loans. Or, a firm might try to capture a monopoly privilege so that it has no competitors at all.

Rent seeking is costly and destructive. Some economists estimate rent seeking destroys 3% of US GNP. Others think it destroys as much as 50% of US GNP. Most estimate the total losses as somewhere in the middle. If they are right, then rent seeking destroys trillions of dollars.[22]

Rent seeking is destructive in part because it stifles innovation. In rent-seeking societies, firms depend on government favor. They

[22] Mueller (2003).

spend money and time seeking favors rather than innovating. The cost of entry into the market grows too high, so that only large, privileged corporations remain.

Consider the problem of occupational licensing. Many states have extensive, expensive, and time-consuming licensing requirements before one can legally braid hat, trim eyebrows, arrange flowers, or do a wide range of other activities. But for such laws, many relatively poor entrepreneurs could have started their own low-overhead businesses. A great number of such laws were nominally created for "protecting the public safety," but, in fact, were created to exclude black people and minorities from these professions.[23]

I don't take this to be a comprehensive list of all the problems with regulation. Obviously, it's not a cost-benefit analysis either, because I haven't gone over all the good things regulations do. My main goal here is just to show that the administrative state is not a free lunch. It has systematic problems and systematic downsides. Many regulations are good in isolation but bad as an aggregate. Some are simply bad.

Private Governance

Here's a joke I see on Reddit and Facebook: "Ayn Rand, Rand Paul, and Paul Ryan walk into a bar. The bartender serves them tainted alcohol because there are no regulations. They die."[24] Apparently, the person making the joke has never bought or sold anything on eBay or Reverb, places that use reputation feedback mechanisms to ensure people do not rip each other off, and which rarely have to call upon help from the government.

This sort of joke reveals how authoritarians and statists tend to think. They assume that in the absence of explicit government regulation, everything will be a disorderly disaster. They tend to have a

[23] Suprenant and Brennan (2020).
[24] https://www.reddit.com/r/Jokes/comments/61y98e/ayn_rand_rand_paul_and_paul_ryan_walk_into_a_bar/.

negative view of human nature, too. They think the only thing stopping people from poisoning each other is a law.

Economist Edward Stringham calls this view "legal centralism," or, more pejoratively, the "Deus Ex Machina theory of law." Legal centralism holds that the "order in the world depends on and is attributable to government law."[25] Now, everyone agrees that *some* order is attributable to government-made law. But legal centralism posits a much stronger claim. On this view, people begin in a sort of primordial legal chaos. Life is nasty, poor, brutish, and short. Law then appears out of the blue, imposed from on high by a protective force, and solves each of these problems.

Legal centrism is empirically false. In fact, most of our legal conventions that are now codified into law arose outside government. In common law countries, such as the United States, England, Canada, and Australia, commercial law, merchant law, property law, and tort law actually did evolve in a polycentric legal system, often outside of and without any backing from governments. These laws governed commercial activity for hundreds of years and were only later adopted by governments. The mass of the body of law that makes Western civilization work *was not*, as a matter of fact, created by governments, and as a matter of fact, it "worked"—it kept order—without government intervention. That is not to say government has no role to play, but at least a great deal of the order we enjoyed did not result from a top-down process of deliberate governmental law-making.

Stringham's more novel point is that government often lacks the ability, knowledge, or incentive to create and enforce good rules that would solve our problems. It is not just that as a matter of fact government did not create and does not enforce many of the rules we live by. Rather, government *will* not and often *cannot* enforce them.

For instance, to take one of Stringham's examples, people rarely defraud each other out of small amounts of money. It is uncommon for, say, my grocery store to cheat me out of a few extra dollars on

[25] Stringham (2015, 5).

my grocery bill. It is tempting to think that what prevents them from cheating me in small amounts is that they know I have recourse to small claims courts, the police, and the like. But that is a mistake. If my grocer cheats me out of $5, I could take him to small claims court, but the cost to me (in terms of court fees, the value of my time, and so on), even if I win, greatly exceeds $5. The transaction costs of *winning* in court exceed the value of the damages. A Hobbesian might conclude that, as a result, people will always cheat each other by small amounts, since the government lacks the capacity to regulate all such instances of fraud and theft, and since the victim lacks the incentive to demand governmental enforcement. But, of course, people rarely cheat each other. Something *other* than government enforcement is doing the trick.

When government cannot or will not solve our problems, we do not immediately fall into chaos. Rather, people generally find *informal* or extra-governmental means to solve problems. They do so because they gain from cooperating with one another. They use reputation effects to govern each other and to incentivize good behavior.

Free Market Welfare States vs. Administrative Welfare States

I think progressives like regulation less than they think they do. My evidence: When progressives and left-liberals describe what they want in a social democracy, they tend to describe the heavily interventionist policies you see in, say, Argentina or Brazil. But when they are asked to point to examples of countries they think are on the right course, they tend to point to countries that are better described as free market welfare states, such as Denmark.

On this point, Table III.3.1 shows the Fraser Institute's 2017 ratings of some of the major social democracies by their degree of freedom from regulation.

Note that the Heritage Institute/*Wall Street Journal* rankings and ratings are very similar. The exact numbers and rankings change year to year, but you probably get the idea.

Table III.3.1 Economic freedom and freedom from regulation

Country	Overall rank	Overall freedom score	Regulation score
Hong Kong	1	8.91	9.44
Singapore	2	8.71	8.98
New Zealand	3	8.50	9.13
Switzerland	4	8.40	8.48
United States	5	8.19	8.86
Ireland	6	8.13	8.39
United Kingdom	7	8.09	8.35
Canada	8	8.08	8.61
Denmark	13	7.89	8.37
Luxembourg	17	7.86	7.88
Japan	17	7.86	8.25
Taiwan	19	7.85	7.64
Germany	20	7.82	8.00
Finland	21	7.80	7.89
Czech Republic	22	7.75	8.19
Iceland	23	7.74	7.68
Netherlands	25	7.72	8.06
Austria	26	7.71	7.45
Norway	32	7.62	7.59
Brazil	120	6.23	4.41
Argentina	146	5.67	5.65

Source: Fraser Institute Economic Freedom Index, 2017. https://www.fraserinstitute.org/economic-freedom/dataset?geozone=world&year=2017&page=dataset&min-year=2&max-year=0&filter=0&sort-field=summary_index&sort-reversed=1

It's difficult to specify what the optimal level of regulation is. I suspect libertarians and classical liberals are too quick to say that we should rely on courts and tort law to fix harms rather than regulation. Now, I am not particularly sanguine about bureaucrats' and regulators' incentives to select the optimal level of regulation. I think they are overly cautious, tend to fail cost-benefit analysis, tend to ignore "unseen" downside harms that the average person who lacks social scientific training cannot easily trace back to them, and also enable and encourage tremendous rent seeking. The countries that need the most regulation, due to lower generalized social trust, also are the countries that will have the worst offending regulators for that same reason.

But, at the same time, these worries also apply to courts, judges, and juries. On certain margins, they may be a bit worse and on others a bit better. Nevertheless—and this is a concession to Arneson's side—when classical liberals say, for example, "Instead of having heavy-handed safety regulations, we should facilitate allowing people to sue manufacturers more easily," they are still largely relying on the state to rescue people from unsafe products. A better strategy for classical liberals, I think, is to do what Stringham does above: show that most useful governance that regulates manufacturer behavior comes from market competition and private means rather than through torts.

At any rate, my main point in this brief section is not to settle this debate once and for all. It's to call attention to the fact that the more successful, richer social democracies are also quite high on the index of economic freedom. They have administrative states, but these states are fairly constrained.

Summary

Social democracy is overrated. It is not the kind, gentle form of capitalism, one that shares and spreads the wealth. Rather, social democracy serves the rich. It mostly provides social insurance to help the rich insulate themselves from some of the risks of markets. It "spreads the wealth" not the poor, but from the very rich to the merely rich. The amount of genuine redistribution is small.

If we genuinely wanted to help the genuinely poor, we would strongly favor open borders and free trade rules that foster increased worldwide economic growth over the fortress welfare states. A more classical liberal/libertarian/laissez-faire capitalist system would do far more to reduce serious poverty and inequality, while social democracies in fact reinforce poverty and inequality.

Finally, while there is a legitimate role for government regulation, we should be cautious. Regulation often fails to make things better and often makes things worse. Rather than being used to protect our children from corporations, regulation is often the very weapon corporations use against them. We should note that the best functioning social democracies—though they fall very far short of the demands of justice—are nevertheless largely open, mostly free to very free market economies, while the highly regulated states are also worse functioning.

PART IV
ARNESON RESPONSE TO BRENNAN

Does Global Justice Oppose Nordic Social Democracy?

Jason Brennan holds that the issue of migration and open borders is a huge plate-glass window through which we cannot but see that social democracy in rich countries is unsupportable in our present world. At least, from a wide range of left-wing and egalitarian positions, social democracy must be rejected if maintenance of social democracy in practical terms is incompatible with implementing open borders, and it may well be that this conflict is sharp, and in fact, we can choose either social democracy or open borders but not both. So urges Brannan.

Brennan is making a nice debater's point here. He himself affirms a right-wing and inegalitarian morality, and from that standpoint, there will be ample grounds for discarding social democracy—especially the generous Nordic social democracy I defend. Moreover, right-wingers would defend open borders for their own reasons, which he articulates. So in this initial chapter, he is arguing in an ecumenical spirit, in effect, that left-wingers and right-wingers alike should be united in marching under the banner, "Down with social democracy!" at least if an undeniably just migration policy requires dismantling generous welfare states.

Debating Capitalism. Richard J. Arneson and Jason Brennan, Oxford University Press.
 DOI: 10.1093/9780190076467.003.0013

Left-wingers with egalitarian leanings should shrug off Brennan's welcoming embrace. From a global justice perspective, "open borders" is not the panacea Brennan makes it out to be.

Brennan boils down his objection to social democracy to a succinct comment: "social democracies are not an effective way of spreading the wealth and ensuring that both rich and poor benefit from capitalist markets. Rather they exclude and harm the genuinely poor, all for the purpose of sharing the wealth between the extremely rich and the merely rich."

In reply, Brennan's objection intertwines two complaints. Neither one has merit. One thought is that bringing about shifts in resources and life prospects between the rich and the poor in rich countries such as Sweden is a trivial matter—restricts individual liberties for no real moral gain. This makes light of the very significant gap between a millionaire and someone struggling to get by on an income of say $15,000 a year. Yes, those standardly classified as poor in rich countries at present are better off than hunter-gatherers, but so what? All else equal, bringing it about that someone living a grim life is enabled to get some decent fulfillment, enjoy some real freedom to live as she chooses, at modest cost to people who by comparison are rolling in dough such as Jason Brennan and I, is from the moral standpoint a big deal improvement. To illustrate, fixing someone's broken leg that would otherwise go untreated is not rendered a moral "Don't care" by the fact that there are people in the world with two broken legs that are not getting treated.

This point becomes stronger when we reflect that money income is a very rough indicator of well-being. So is relative poverty—being worse off than others in the society you inhabit. But unchosen relative poverty correlates with not being able to participate fully in the way of life of fellow members of your community, and this outsider status does, for many, become a serious obstacle to fulfillment. Moreover, in the United States at least, since the 1980s, wages have barely risen at all for those with a high school education and no more, even though economic growth has been good. The result is that many people, college-educated and better off, see their lives and the lives of their children improving, while ordinary workers see their condition stagnating. This perception of being left behind is a kick in the teeth. In the Nordic social democracies, with generous welfare states, relative poverty has not increased in this way. Dismissing this as a gain accruing to the merely rich—to whom, presumably, we owe nothing—is dead wrong from an egalitarian/prioritarian standpoint. Even though helping the global poor is more important than helping better off but still badly off fellow countrymen, the latter still matters. Also, we might be exaggerating the inefficacy of egalitarian transfers within rich countries as a means to boost global equality. Angus Deaton, focusing on the US situation, suggests that if we identify quality of life not just with one's material condition but also broader factors, some poor people in rich countries will qualify as members of the global poor (Deaton 2013, 2023; Case and Deaton 2023).

In this connection, Brennan makes a further interesting claim—interesting but false. This is that in rich countries, those who end up at the bottom largely have only themselves to blame. It has been pointed out that in the United States, if teenagers would finish high school, get a full-time job, and delay getting married and having children until 21 years of age, their chances of ending up poor would be negligible. Accepting this statement, what is false is the further claim that the rich country poor are on the whole mostly sufficiently responsible for their plight as to extinguish obligations to aid them.

I agree that, in principle, we should give priority to bringing about gains for a person, the more morally deserving the individual is, along with priority for the person, the worse in absolute terms is the life the person is heading for. (How relevant this idea is to public policy choice is debatable, since public policy attempts to distinguish the more from the less deserving are costly to implement and likely unreliable at best.) But the key is that we need to employ a sensible standard for being morally deserving or undeserving. The more difficult and painfully costly it is to try to do what's right the more credit you get if you try, and the less discredit accrues to you if you don't. By this standard, people like me who have been lucky in life and nonetheless have been assholes sometimes can be less morally deserving than people who have had piles of bad luck beyond their power to control dumped on them, struggle against these pressures, and ultimately mess up by gross imprudence or immorality.

So far I have replied to the first of Brennan's two strikes against rich country social democracy. His second strike is that closing their national borders to migrants and blocking the freedom of people anywhere on Earth to settle and resettle wherever they choose, so long as they violate no one's private property rights, is a massive violation of our global justice obligations.

Here's the gist of this second strike argument: Redistributing income from the very rich to the merely rich in rich countries is far less important than gaining improvements in the incomes of the global poor. Rich countries can effectively promote income growth of the global poor by opening their borders to migration without limit, including accepting would-be poor migrants. The incomes of the poor migrants would shoot up, and by remitting much of their income windfall to poor relatives in their home country, the migrants would be spreading the income redistribution to great effect. It may be that opening borders would not cause significant economic losses to "poor" citizens of rich countries, but even if it did, opening the borders is still the right course. Furthermore, current attitude shifts among voters in rich countries suggest that a majority of voters in presently generous (Nordic) social democracies will fear the cultural disruptions of massive in-migration and fear that the in-migration of the global poor will cause swift erosion of popular support for the now heavily burdened welfare state, leading to its erosion and disappearance. Foreseeing this, less wealthy citizens in Nordic social democracies will oppose open borders or anything close to that, to preserve the current social democracy regime. Hence global justice in practical terms is directly in conflict with maintenance of generous welfare state policies in rich countries.

Let's accept that in Nordic social democracies, for the present, open borders and maintenance of social democratic regimes are in conflict. The issue then becomes, which to choose?

We should agree with global justice cosmopolitanism. This doctrine says that each person is fundamentally a citizen of the world, and that what we owe morally to others by way of consideration and concern is not in itself affected by impersonal social relationships, including shared membership in an ethnic group, race, sex (being a man or a woman), gender, national community, or nation-state. (But IF we have special duties of fair play toward cooperating fellow countrymen, that would strengthen the case for the acceptability of social democracy.)

The critic of social democracy holds that absent introducing open borders, rich countries nowadays cannot fulfill their global justice duties to contribute their fair share to income improvement in the living conditions of the global poor. Simplifying, let's identify these global justice duties with quickly reducing global greenhouse gas emissions to net zero to save the planet while simultaneously facilitating rapid economic development in poor countries. This is the global egalitarian case for open borders. Moreover, we should all acknowledge that there is anyway a strong basic libertarian right of any person to move anywhere on Earth where one can find an employer willing to offer employment and a property owner willing to rent or sell access to housing. Just as we all accept a strong moral right to free movement and resettling within any country, we should accept the same right extends across national borders. So urges the critic.

In reply, one consideration is that the gain from open borders may not be as huge as Brennan imagines. Social scientists note that we cannot extrapolate from the expectation that there will be gains from moderate increases in poor people's migration into rich countries to a confident expectation that massive increases in such migration would have desirable effects overall taking into account the costs and benefits falling on all globally affected persons. We just don't know (Hanson 2009, Collier 2013).

More important, Brennan takes it for granted there is a strong within-country libertarian moral right to settle and resettle wherever one pleases (without violating others' rights by trespassing on their private property or the like). He then asserts that this basic moral right to free migration applies across national borders. But we should deny the starting premise. I deny that I have a basic moral right to resettle as I choose within my country any more than I have a basic moral right to drive as I please regardless of the costs my driving imposes on others. (Suppose San Diego becomes very congested, and only employed commuters and others with special needs are permitted to drive on major traffic arteries during rush hours. This seems OK, depending on a moralized cost and benefit assessment.) If I have a moral right here, it is to decent life prospects, and having wide freedom to resettle usually enhances my life prospects. Same holds across borders. Living in the United States, I have no basic moral right to settle wherever I might please, in Switzerland, Israel, or Singapore. My resettling may impose costs and benefits on many people, including those less well off than I am.

A yet more consequential point is that fully open borders, even if desirable, would be utterly utopian, just in the sense that rich country voters will reject it. Nor will rich country dictators go for it. So let's attend to politically feasible rich country policy choices that would partly fulfill their global justice duties. For any global justice gains that an attainable loosening of immigration restrictions in a rich country could bring about, with the side effect of ending the Nordic social democratic regime in that country, there will be a morally superior attainable alternative, that substitutes rich country donation of cash and capital to people in globally poor countries for opening borders. This always available alternative is morally superior because it would more fairly divide the costs of fulfillment of global justice among rich and poor in wealthy countries. Roughly, tax the rich and use the proceeds to send cash and nuclear power plants and clean technology to very poor countries with functioning state capacity. Help poor countries themselves to become low-income versions of Nordic social democracies. Possible long-term declines in rich countries' economic growth that such capital transfer would bring about can be more than offset by increases in long-term now-poor countries' economic growth.

Here's an analogy to illustrate the argument I am advancing. Imagine that in a land with extremely cold winters, very poor homeless people—in no way responsible for their plight—are shivering and in danger of freezing. One simple policy response would be to require the poor neighbors of the very poor to take them into their homes and shelter them each winter. An alternative policy that more fairly shares the burden of ameliorating the condition of the very poor is to impose taxes on all of us, with heavier taxes on the rich, the funds to be used to provide seasonal shelter to those specially in need. A complementary policy would be to ban local zoning ordinances that make it impossible to build affordable housing and that drive up the prices of the homes of well-off homeowners. We should choose policies that fairly share the burdens of helping the truly needy. Brennan's suggested cure for global poverty looks appealing only if we ignore the imperative of fair burden-sharing.

Objection: Capital transfer from rich countries to poor countries will not help the global poor as effectively as opening borders to migration. For example, foreign aid will end up in the pockets of poor country rulers. Reply: Foreign aid on the part of rich nations has mostly been driven by big-power rivalries and rich country domestic politics. The history does not show that feasible aid efforts sensibly motivated cannot succeed. We should channel aid toward poor countries with the capacity and political will to absorb it to the benefit of their poor members.

Does the Imperative of Growth Conflict with Social Democratic Redistribution?

Brennan argues that redistribution (almost always) conflicts with economic growth, and economic growth from any sensible moral perspective is the better choice. As he puts it, dividing and redividing the presently existing pie of resources does not do anything to produce a bigger and better pie of resources over a single person's lifetime much less over the long run of successive generations. Market exchange in a framework of private ownership of resources is the engine of economic growth. Governmental redistribution diverts resources from growth-enhancing uses and dampens the incentives of rich and poor alike to be productive. He asserts, "We face a dilemma: Some things we might do to reduce the burdens of poverty today come at the expense of ending poverty tomorrow."

In reply: growth versus redistribution is a false dilemma. Some forms of redistribution are growth-enhancing. Moreover the forms of redistribution that empirical evidence shows to be growth-enhancing are conspicuously those that Nordic social democracies characteristically implement. This is true both on the side of choices of how to tax to gather funds for public spending and on the side of choices of what types of pro-poor spending to select. On the spending side, public funding of education for children and youth has high payoff for their future productivity and well-being. Over their lifetime, that benefits those who interact with them also. The same is true for pre-school high-quality day care. Policies such as a year's paid parental leave following childbirth, subsidized toddler day care, and affordable high-quality after-school care for primary school children make it easier for parents of young children—especially women—to sustain jobs and career. This is good for growth, and also reduces the oppression of women in patriarchal families. Policies that especially enhance the skills of children born to fewer advantages compress the distribution of people's market earnings over their lives, and also contribute to growth and to everyone's expected prosperity over the long run.

Wage setting institutions in the Nordic countries also play a "predistributive" equalizing role. These involve collective bargaining between unions representing employees and associations representing employers for large sectors of the economy. These institutions give employees more bargaining power than they would have under more local bargaining, and arguably shift the sharing of profits across firm stakeholders without impeding efficiency.

The considerations above speak to the puzzle: How do Nordic social democracies maintain high taxes without compromising economic growth and long-term prosperity. The puzzle is not, do they manage this trick. They do. The question is how they do it. Looking at OECD countries after 1945, an economist and historian of public spending summarizes the evidence: "Within the range of true historical experience, there is no clear net GDP cost of higher social transfers" (Lindert 2004, see also Kenworthy 2020).

Further on how to make the distribution of opportunities more fair (equal) without undue efficiency loss: Rather than simply transfer money from those who have more to those who have less, we might also provide some goods for all. If public provision of some goods is more efficient than letting the market do its thing, and if some types of goods, though beneficial for all, especially boost the well-being of the poor, in-kind provision can be both equalizing and efficient. This applies to provision of insurance against unsought unemployment and active labor market policies that facilitate retraining of those who have lost jobs and matching of individuals to employment opportunities, health care to protect against threats to continued good health and long life, and old age pensions. In-kind provision of specific types of benefits has a paternalistic flavor, echoed in the negative description of social democratic welfare states as "cradle to grave socialism." Why not limit redistribution among adults to transfer of money to those who have less of it, so recipients can spend it as they choose? Reply: Sometimes, overriding an individual's own judgment about what will be best for him really advances his welfare, and then, paternalism is OK.

On the side of gathering funds for public spending, European social democracies tend to rely more than other countries on taxes on consumption (e.g., value-added tax—VAT). These are easy to collect and hard to evade. If consumption taxes include "sin" taxes on behavior that either imposes costs on nonconsenting others or qualifies as nonvirtuous imprudent choice, for example, consumption of alcohol, cigarettes, and gasoline, they will be especially mild in the deadweight inefficiency costs they carry with them that retard growth. Payroll taxes, also relied on heavily by Nordic states, have the quality of being easy to collect and hard to evade. Tax rates are high in the Nordic countries, but not progressive. As your income rises, your tax rate does not increase. Such taxes may also minimize deadweight losses of redistribution.

Why redistribute at all? Many of us believe, it would be wrong for me to forcibly take resources from Sally and redistribute them to someone I regard as more in need of resources or more deserving of good fortune. What holds for me holds for others as well. Why is it morally OK for the state to behave in a similar way?

Several reasons combine here. The simplest is that if all are bound by moral duties to help the worse off, state coercion can give all of us the assurance that all who should be helping are doing so. Even if private charity could satisfy the need, the burden of helping would be lopsidedly unfairly shared, and anyway private charity absent state action would not fill the need. Nor would private vigilante action substitute for even-handed state action. (In the Robin Hood myth, these problems do not arise. Robin Hood and his band enjoy their work, target their robbery effectively at the undeserving rich, and give judiciously to the poor according to their needs.)

Contrary to those who hold that private ownership rights are semi-sacred, a better view is that private ownership rights are tools to bring about morally better outcomes. They work well in many circumstances, and the benefits of private ownership significantly depend on security of ownership. If your land might be taken from you at any moment, it is likely of little use to you. These are weighty considerations. But circumstances vary, and changes can weaken or extinguish private ownership rights. Private ownership always has a stewardship element, as John Locke already had noted in 1687. If your continued enjoyment of ownership does not serve the common good, it lapses.

Private takings standardly have significant downsides. They tend to erode the rule of law, which tends to engender greater social justice fulfillment even in significantly unjust societies. A bunch of people acting on their private beliefs does not add up to coherent policy. In contrast, redistributive takings that are democratically authorized and that conform to rule of law requirements are less likely to exhibit these flaws. For these reasons, state action taking property from the rich and generally well off and redistributing it to those who are poor, especially through no fault of their own, and generally badly off overall in lifetime well-being prospects, can be morally justified even when a bunch of private forcible takings that by sheer coincidence resulted in identical losses for some and gains for others would be unjustified.

There are further twists to growth versus redistribution. If we anticipate that on the whole succeeding generations of people will be better off than the present generation, that is a reason to favor somewhat boosting conditions for overall worse-off present people, giving priority to the worse off among them. Some dampening of growth may be morally required. But in any event, economic growth will not continue indefinitely, and anyway should not. To illustrate the issue, suppose that to enjoy decent lives on Earth, people must have access to clean water, breathable air, and arable land. Future technological improvements will improve our capacity to get these basic resources from available natural resources, but at some level of depletion of resources, technological improvements won't be able to outpace the depletion. Suppose that if population stabilizes at some high level, and depletion of resources is controlled so technological gains offset it, human life can be sustained at a high level of population and very good lives for all far into the distant future—perhaps for hundreds of millions of years. A no-growth society would then be needed for a sustainable, morally best long-term outcome.

Should We Downsize the Administrative State, Doing Away with Social Democracy?

In Chapter III.3, Brennan criticizes social democracy on the grounds that it tends toward a big state—one that imposes high taxes on citizens, does too much, and overregulates. His first shot at supporting this suspicion of the administrative state is to rehearse the familiar right-wing objection to the inference from a showing of some market economy failure to a conclusion to the effect that we ought in this circumstance to implement a state policy that seeks to correct the problem. This inference is indeed fallacious. From the fact that the market economy generates objectionable outcomes, it does not follow that we should use state power to try to correct the problem. The remedy we deploy may expectably fail to alleviate the problem, or the cure may be worse than the disease.

The same point applies to failures of state action as well From the sheer fact that state action is going awry and messing up people's lives in some way, it does not follow that leaving this matter to people's individual marketplace choices would bring about better results at acceptable cost. Sometimes, the only workable fix for bad state action is better state action, which we ought to be working with others to secure. For example, congestion at rush hours on freeways and roads in metropolitan areas of the United States is a big problem. It doesn't follow that abandoning government regulation of roadways and letting people drive as they choose would be a good idea.

The state and the market economy, when both are functioning well, are complements, not substitutes. What the state does adds benefit that the market economy is not well-suited to produce. For this reason, the basic drift of Brennan's challenges to the administrative state starts from misunderstanding. The mistaken presumption is that if we just got the state out of the way, the actions of private individuals, each acting voluntarily and pragmatically, will expectably better solve the problems for which people look to the state for solutions.

The market economy tends to undersupply public goods, understood as goods such that with respect to a group of people (a) if some consume some of the good, none can feasibly be excluded from consuming some of it, and (b) consumption of some of the good by one person leaves none the less available for the consumption of it by others. By coercing all group members to contribute to the production of such goods, when they are truly good and worth their cost, the state can bring it about that we are all better off.

An important instance is reduction in people's risk of suffering death by violence over the course of their lives. In nonstate societies for which we have evidence, the risk of violent death is about five times higher or more than in societies with a state (that claims and mostly effectively enforces a monopoly on the use of force and violence.) Moreover, in Western Europe since the rise of the centralized state (1600–2000), rates of homicide have steadily dropped, and risk of death from violent attacks of all sorts overall (including in war!) have likewise declined steadily. In Western Europe, Australia, Canada, and the United States (countries for which we have good data), over the last 50 years there have been large declines in rape and violence against women and lynchings and racial pogroms, along with steady increases in people's attitudes of toleration, leading to policies protective of outsiders, marginalized folk, adherents of diverse ways of life. These are further rights advances for which "a competent government and police force and a dependable infrastructure for trade and commerce," reducing chronic violence, are prerequisites (Pinker 2011, 313).

Brennan is not denying that some level of state administration and regulation is needed for a market economy to deliver prosperity and good life prospects in our world. His assertion is that citizens in social democracies, including the Nordics, are living under bloated states, and that would be better off—more prosperous and free—living in states that are far closer to laissez-faire than social democratic.

Brennan and I read the relevant social science differently. The best available social science rightly interpreted will sort this out. Our disagreements also involve moral disagreements. Let's try to clarify these.

Concerning liberty, our disagreement is not whether liberty is important to protect, but why and what kind. Every adult person is ordinarily better placed than others to have sound beliefs about the personal matters that bear on that very person's best choice of life plan. When your choices mainly affect yourself, others are rarely in a position override your judgment. When your decisions affect others besides yourself, without their consent, the presumption that we should let the person act as she chooses no longer holds.

Brennan states, "*Liberal* political philosophies hold that liberty is the fundamental value which states must respect." I'd put the idea less narrowly. Cass Sunstein stipulates that liberals believe in "freedom, human rights, pluralism, security, the rule of law, and democracy." Liberalism on this broad view is a big tent. Those inside it might value freedom and the other things on the list for their own sakes or as means to further more fundamental values or as some mixture. To be a liberal, you value these things a lot, but not unconditionally.

Brennan holds that any proposal for government regulation must overcome a high bar of justification, on the grounds that the presumption must be, individual liberty takes priority. He adds that the economic liberties are liberties on par with others. Hence, those who argue for state restriction of economic liberty on the basis that the unfettered free market leads to some undesirable outcomes but who would balk at a parallel argument for state regulation of our freedom to have sex with willing partners or of our freedom of speech are arguing inconsistently.

However, not everything that can be called a liberty is a big deal. There's no inconsistency in holding that some level of regulation of products offered for sale in the marketplace is acceptable but that comparable regulation of people's freedom to decide whom to seek out as friends or romantic partners, or whether to devote themselves to skiing or surfing or playing video games, or which clubs or churches or other associations to join would be completely unacceptable. The costs and benefits of regulations of these different kinds of activity are different. The welfarist egalitarian will hold that the optimal regulatory regime is the one that best promotes people's welfare fairly distributed. This principle can justify different degrees of protection of different kinds of freedom.

Brennan has the hunch that when people's actions have spillover costs falling on others, those affected will informally negotiate and find accommodation, leading to new social norms and reasonable adjustments, without state regulation. Maybe. But the adjustments may reflect the balance of social power, not justice. Democratic voting, history shows, can improve on raw behavioral adjustments. Also, when people make huge self-harming mistakes, which restriction of their liberty against their will would prevent, do they have a right against paternalistic restriction come what may?

A rigid antipaternalist stance will work fine for the good choosers of the world; a perfectly prudent well-informed person will never be made better off by restriction of her freedom for her own good. For the rest of us, a little judicious paternalism can help a lot, and even be lifesaving. As the Beatles song lyric has it, "I get by with a little help from my friends." Add that on the whole and on the average, good choosers are more likely to be successful, wealthy, and better off in well-being prospects. So the paternalism issue poses a conflict of interest between better offs and worse offs: This is because we cannot always have different rules for good and bad choosers, and in some contexts it would be wrongly stigmatizing to impose such rules. Putting it aggressively, I would say rigid antipaternalism is an unfair ideology of the good choosers—accepting some limited paternalism would be a boon to worse offs. This matters for the assessment of social democracy. Think of generous welfare state policies as the extension of a helping hand to people who especially need it.

PART V
BRENNAN RESPONSE TO ARNESON

Arneson's Approach

I commend Arneson's philosophical methods. Arneson recognizes that we cannot defend institutions simply by defending the particular moral goals, principles, or outcomes various outcomes we *want* those institutions to achieve. We instead need to show that any particular set of institutions actually succeeds in delivering those things, and further does so better than the alternatives. Many philosophers (despite years of training) and most laypeople skip this second step.

To illustrate the mistake (which Arneson avoids), consider this bad argument.

1. It's good if no one goes hungry.
2. Socialist institutions aim to ensure no one goes hungry.
3. Therefore, we should have socialism.

The problem with this argument is that even if premises 1 and 2 are true, 3 doesn't follow. One reason it doesn't follow is that it's an empirical question whether socialism of any particular sort in any particular context actually provides people with enough to eat, and whether it does so better than other systems. (And it turns out socialism is quite bad at getting people fed.)

Debating Capitalism. Richard J. Arneson and Jason Brennan, Oxford University Press.
 DOI: 10.1093/9780190076467.003.0014

Now, consider the following argument. See if you can spot the same mistake:

1. Suppose, for the sake of argument, that the purpose of government is to promote the general welfare.
2. Therefore, the government ought to have a robust welfare state with guaranteed minimum incomes and automatic transfers of wealth to all adults.

Again, problem with this argument is that even granting the premise (1), the conclusion (2) does not *follow*. We cannot *infer* the conclusion from the premise.

Further, there's an ambiguity about what it means to "aim." Any outcome a government should "aim" to promote can be achieved through either direct or indirect means. The government might attempt to promote welfare *directly*, by instituting welfare offices, offering subsidies and grants, providing a basic income, subsidizing employment, attempting macroeconomic adjustments, offering free health care, and the like. Alternatively, the government might promote welfare goals *indirectly*, by providing a basic institutional framework (such as the rule of law, representative democracy, courts, and a well-functioning property rights regime) under which people will spontaneously act so as to promote the general welfare. It's an open, empirical question whether various direct or indirect means work best. Arneson and I both agree that this indirect methods in fact produce a high level of welfare. We disagree about the extent to which direct methods should supplement the indirect.

Many works of political philosophy compare *idealized* description of the author's favored institutions to realistic descriptions of the institutions they dislike. For instance, G. A. Cohen defends socialism not by showing socialism works better than capitalism in the real world (indeed, he more or less admits it does not), but by comparing idealized socialism in which people behave exactly as he wishes they did to what he takes to be realistic account of capitalism, where people behave the way your neighbors do. He thinks this somehow shows that socialism is morally superior to capitalism, tout court.[1] John Rawls says utopian anarchism cannot work because people are too selfish to contribute to public goods. Yet, when he defends his favored form of government, he explicitly asks us to imagine that people are always motivated to do what's just.[2]

Arneson avoids such mistakes. When theorizing about institutions, he thinks we must be consistent in the constraints we work with. If our goal is to describe a morally perfect and ideally just society, then we are free to imagine radical changes in human motivation. After all, in morally perfect and perfectly just societies, everyone is morally perfect and perfectly just. Many institutions, such as criminal courts, the military, or the police, exist only to deal with wrongdoing; morally perfect people would have no need of such institutions, and so those institutions would not exist in ideally just societies.[3] On the other hand, if we want to make recommendations about which institutions are best for the real world, we must consider how real people behave inside such institutions. Institutions fit for angels might be unfit for real people.

Arneson and I agree that what he calls "socialist principles" are best obtained, in the real world, by some form of capitalism. Real people are neither nice nor smart enough to make genuine socialism work on a mass scale. Implementing genuine socialism undermines rather than promotes "socialist" goals. It's an interesting question whether morally perfect angels would be socialist, but that's not our question here.[4]

That said, I am unsure whether we should label Arneson's favored principles "socialist." I worry that this invites confusion. I don't want to call concern for personal autonomy or consent "capitalist" nor do I want to call concern to prevent economic domination "socialist." These are things anyone can and should care about. It's an open question which institutions best realize or promote these values given any set of background constraints. Still, Arneson's point is that the socialism is not an end in itself, but at best a means to an end.

[1] Cohen (2009).
[2] Rawls (2001, 137).
[3] Cohen (2009); Brennan and Freiman (2022).
[4] See Cohen (2009) and Brennan (2024).

Why the Global Perspective Matters More than the Nationalist Perspective

Arneson makes a strong pitch for how wonderful Denmark is . . . for the Danish. I admit I am not convinced social democratic capitalism is better than other forms of capitalism, even from the narrow perspective of economic nationalism. But, as readers say, my main worry is that prioritarianism and egalitarianism *inside* rich countries matter little, even from and perhaps especially from a left-wing point of view. What matters is the global perspective.

Let me add two analogies to reinforce what I've already argued. In both analogies, I will ask you to imagine that rich, privileged groups practice redistribution *inside* their group but do nothing for the genuinely worst off, who are outside the group. How should prioritarians or egalitarians react?

First, consider that many wealthy families practice a degree of internal socialism. Rich parents and grandparents funnel resources toward their children and grandchildren. They purchase elite education, piano and lacrosse lessons, SAT and math tutoring, all to develop their children's human capital. They buy their children's first houses or cars, help them start businesses, and bequeath them money upon death. Rich families work to ensure family members live autonomous, self-directed lives free of domination. Many rich families act as if they read and follow Arneson's "socialist values" from his Chapter II.3, but only *inside* the family.

Yet socialists have traditionally been critical of such rich families, and families in general, because of their internal socialism, not despite it.[5] Sure, they say, internal family socialism inside wealth families increases equality and promotes welfare *inside* individual families, but that's just the privileged privileging the privileged, the rich helping the rich. Socialists and egalitarians generally believe that internal family socialism undermines socialist and egalitarians goals

[5] For what it's worth, one major exception is Miller (2001). Miller thinks this internal egalitarianism is the main principle of justice inside families, while societies as a whole should follow meritocratic rather than egalitarian norms.

at the national level. They think that rich parents who purchase SAT prep classes or help their kids start businesses thereby harm poor kids who cannot compete. (Arneson himself defends a principle of equal opportunity for welfare, so he shares some such worries.)

For these reasons, many past and some present radical socialists wanted to abolish the family. Today, more moderate leftists and egalitarians instead want to limit parental transfers of wealth, perhaps by forbidding inheritance or limiting how much money parents can gift to their children.[6] They also want to "compensate" for unearned family advantages, "undeserved inequalities," and being "born into less favorable social positions."[7] Both the radicals and the moderates view the internal socialism of rich families as a threat to their ideals.

Suppose I announced that I am an egalitarian or prioritarian, but my egalitarianism and prioritarianism apply only to families. Suppose I said that in my theory, the locus of social justice is the family. Suppose I claim families should realize what Arneson calls "socialist values," but the gaps between people in different families are of tertiary moral significance at best. "Leftism inside families but not between them" is my slogan. Socialists would think this theory makes a mockery of their concerns.

For the sake of intellectual consistency, I would expect leftist, socialist-leaning egalitarians to extend these same kinds of worries about internal socialism, or social democracy, of rich countries full of rich citizens. Socialists and social democrats must explain why the locus of social justice concerns is the nation-state, as opposed to something more local or something more global. They need to explain why the GINI coefficients of Denmark, the United States, and Haiti are primary matters, but why the global GINI coefficient is of secondary, tertiary, or no concern. "Leftism inside nations but not between them" is their slogan, but I think this makes a mockery of their concerns.

[6] For example, see Halliday (2018).

[7] Rawls (1999a, 86).

Griping about income inequality among Americans or the Danish often seems like griping about income inequality among the Vanderbilts. Maybe it matters, but it's of tertiary concern at best. As I explained briefly in my own chapters, most Americans born into "poverty" can more or less guarantee that they will become the American "middle class" so long as they exercise minimal prudence.[8] I put "poverty" and "middle class" in scare quotes because, as I discussed previously and will discuss more below, "poverty" by American standards is better than middle class by world standards, "middle class" by American standards is wealthy by world standards.

Let's consider a second metaphor. Imagine there are a number of elite colleges, called Birthright Harvard, Birthright Princeton, Birthright Yale, and so on. Imagine all of the following are true:

- Nearly all of their graduates enjoy high incomes, economic security, personal freedom and autonomy, fulfilling jobs free of domination, just gender relations, and other "socialist" values.
- Nearly all students come from privileged backgrounds.
- Each university has significant internal redistribution and "predistribution," where rich alumni share their wealth to ensure all other students and other alumni do well.
- Admission to Birthright Harvard, etc., is determined almost entirely by legacy status. Alumni children are automatically admitted, regardless of merit.
- However, each year, the Birthright schools also admit a few exceptional meritorious students from outside the legacy pool. These merit-admits constitute about 1% of the admissions pools each year.
- For the most part, the majority of legacy students resent the minority merit admits. Legacy students claim the merit admits harm the school, even though the statistics show the opposite.

[8] See also Brennan (2022).

- Pace these students, economists at Birthright Harvard, Birthright Princeton, and other elite birthright universities, have produced ample research showing that the legacy students would actually be better off if the universities admitted far more students from outside the legacy pool. Indeed, many claim that the schools would benefit from having close to open admissions. These new admits would be much, much better off too.
- If Birthright Harvard had open admissions or admitted far more merit-based students, it could not afford to continue its internal redistribution. Still, it would *need* it less, because almost everyone would be better off.
- Current legacy students nevertheless say that they only care about social justice among legacy students. They think outsiders are of tertiary concern.

That's how it goes for Birthright Harvard, Birthright Princeton, and about 25 or so of their peers. What about other students?

- Students who do not attend the top 25 birthright universities usually have much worse lives, no matter how prudently they act. While legacy students who attend Birthright Harvard tend to have wonderful lives even if they are unconscientious and imprudent, students at Birthright Fitchburg State and Birthright UMass Boston tend to have much worse outcomes. That's largely because these other birthright universities have bad leadership who mistreat and exploit students. Still, everyone attends some college or other because nonattendance is even worse. (Note: I am not saying actual Fitchburg State or UMass Boston are like this. This is just a thought experiment.)

If real-world universities worked this way (and to some extent they do), they'd be repugnant from an egalitarian, welfarist, or left-wing point of view, despite their *internal* egalitarianism and prioritarianism. Birthright Harvard realizes "socialist values" among privileged people but ignores the worst off. A left-wing person could defend them only if (pace the economics department) there are no feasible alternatives. But modern social democracies are analogous to these Birthright colleges.

Arguments from analogy work only as well as the analogies hold. But in this case, the problem with my analogies is that they go too *easy* on social democracies. From the standpoint of social justice, social democracy is far more repugnant than these analogies suggest. Personally, I think families have the prerogative, and often the obligation, to prioritize family members over strangers, even when those strangers are far needier. In partnerships, cooperatives, and corporations, people voluntarily join their rightful property for a common cause. This also gives them some leeway and prerogative. My pool club has no duty to redistribute our resources to needier pool clubs. But social democratic nation-states are not like families, partnerships, cooperatives, or corporations. They are involuntary, distal collections of strangers bound by loose legal and (sometimes) cultural connections of far less moral significance. It's thus *easier* to defend redistribution inside families and Birthright Harvard than inside nation-states.

Feasibility

Arneson seems to agree. He says:

> On the face of it, widening the scope of application of justice requirements from within one's own country to the entire Earth (or beyond) entirely unsettles the assessment of Nordic social democracy (Milanovic 2019, 129–136). A rich country's implementing and sustaining social democracy institutions has no inherent tendency to be doing the best it can to contribute to fulfillment of justice worldwide. After all, those classified as poor in one's rich country might turn out to be classified as well off, not poor at all in a global ranking. At least, this is uncontroversially so if socialist values include a significant welfarist egalitarian component. One country's fulfilling these socialist values internally does not say anything about whether it contributes to global fulfillment of these values to any degree.

Arneson admits that open migration and an open labor market would likely serve the world's poor far better than anything else. However, he worries that it is infeasible.[9]

Whether something is feasible depends on which sense of "feasible" in mind. The significance of the objection changes too.

One sense of infeasible is *physically impossible*. For instance, it's infeasible for me to bench press the moon—I literally can't do it. This sense of infeasibility matters in political philosophy because you can have an obligation to do something only if you can do it.

But Arneson denies that open borders are infeasible in this sense. Countries could open borders if they wanted to. Many had open borders in the past. Asking a country to have more open admissions is not like asking it to bench press the moon.

Consider a second sense of infeasible: A policy might be infeasible in the sense that it's *not currently on current agenda*; it's not something people will likely vote for tomorrow. On this new sense of "infeasible," a policy could function just fine if implemented, but it's unlikely anyone will implement it. (Perhaps they aren't aware of the policy, or they are misinformed about its efficacy.)

This sense of infeasibility is unimportant for philosophers. You wouldn't object to a policy by saying, "That policy would work just fine if we implemented it, but it's infeasible because people don't happen to know about it or support it yet." It would *work*—but it's not *in the works*.

Now consider a more interesting sense of "infeasible": A policy might be infeasible because it requires radical changes in human motivation. Suppose a policy or institution requires people to be much nicer, more altruistic, or more morally motivated than they are. It doesn't require them to behave better than they *could* behave, only better than they *will* behave, given their immoral preferences.

For instance, in a new deleted blog post, the philosopher Joseph Heath complained that libertarianism is a kind of "self-control aristocracy."[10] The libertarians he knows are nearly only highly

[9] For a longer examination of the issue, see Pearson (2023).

[10] Some of the text survives in this response: https://www.libertarianism.org/columns/libertarianisms-untroubling-aristocracy-self-control.

conscientious and responsible people. Indeed, psychological studies confirm this.[11] But, he claims, libertarianism is infeasible because most people are not as responsible and conscientious as libertarians.

World peace and complete military disarmament are probably infeasible in this third sense. In one way, it would be "easy" to achieve world peace: Everyone must merely refuse to initiate violence against others. Still, this doesn't imply that Sweden and Norway should disarm. After all, Russia is right there. Vladimir Putin could do the right thing, but he won't. So, it's not feasible in this third sense to eliminate the military.

This third kind of feasibility is philosophically interesting. It bears on what we should do in the real world, in response to and anticipation of others' wrongdoing.

To defend the social democratic nation-state against me, the best move is to claim that my proposals are infeasible in this third sense. But that's tricky.

One reason it's tricky is because the critic needs to avoid double standards. For instance, sometimes when I argue with Rawlsians or socialists, they tell me open-borders and growth-friendly policies are infeasible (in this third sense). They then go on to explain how instead the United States should undertake a whole range of other radical proposals for the reform or abolition of this institution or that. Their proposed reforms and changes are usually as infeasible (in this third sense) as my own. They treat "infeasible" as if it were a sniper rifle that kills my view, when it's more like a bomb that kills us all.

Arneson avoids this problem in large part because his argument is so conservative. He argues that slightly more social democratic countries (Denmark as it is right now) are better than slightly less social democratic countries (the United States as it is right now). He compares actuals to actuals. However, it's unclear whether the United States *could* be more like Denmark in this third sense of "feasible." If I said Haiti and China should become like Denmark, you would likely object that this is infeasible in this third sense. Maybe

[11] Iyer et al. (2012).

making the United States more like Denmark involves some radical changes in human nature, even though the countries have similar institutions.[12]

Regardless, it's unclear that open immigration or my other proposals are infeasible in this third sense. Consider communitarian socialism as archetype of this third sense of infeasible. Certain forms of communitarian/utopian socialism demand that people become impartial between their own welfare and others, or between the welfare of their children and of strangers. In contrast, the economics of mass migration generally shows that mass migration is a win-win, positive-sum game. New immigrants become rich not at our expense but to our benefit.

One might instead argue that opening borders is infeasible because most people are xenophobic. Perhaps this xenophobia leads to an immigration Laffer Curve: If we allow in too many immigrants, this will enrage the domestic population, who will respond by closing borders even more. On this theory, if you try to get N immigrants, you end up with < N.

Notice that this objection to opening borders is equivalent to saying, in 1955, that we shouldn't desegregate schools too quickly because there will be racist backlash. I'd be surprised if people on the Left found such an objection compelling, even if the empirical claim (that it would cause racist backlash) were true.

Similarly, suppose I argued that we shouldn't increase welfare transfers in the United States because this would cause a Republican backlash. Social democrats would likely be unmoved by this objection, even if I could prove such a backlash would occur. They would say we should overcome or nullify the backlash.

At any rate, it's far from clear that immigration is infeasible in this way. A large body of research on the "contact hypothesis" finds that exposure to immigrants reduces domestic citizens' antipathy toward them.[13] When immigrants move into a country, the people who

[12] Alesina, Glaeser, and Sacerdote (2001).

[13] Gihleb Giuntella, and Stella (2022); Alesina and Tabellini (2024); Ellison et al. (2011); Frølund Thomsen (2012).

actually live and work around the immigrants become more favorable toward them. Most of the xenophobic backlash occurs among citizens who live away from and don't interact with immigrants. This all suggests the solution to xenophobic backlash is not less immigration, but more, and more *widespread*.

Should the United States Be *More* Social Democratic?

Comparing the United States and Denmark is more like comparing cultivars of apples; it's not comparing apples to oranges. Both have market economies that are overall quite free in absolute terms and when compared to the rest of the world. Both have large governments and large welfare and social insurance states. Some Europeans think the United States is "cowboy capitalist" while some Americans think Western Europe is socialist; neither view survives scrutiny.

Still, I'll end by briefly considering whether the United States would be better off (from an internal, nationalist perspective) if its welfare state were more like Denmark's. Answering this question requires us to first answer other complicated questions. For instance, when assessing what counts as a robust welfare state, do we look at outcomes, or percent GDP spent, or something else? Or, consider: Are European welfare states in effect subsidized by the American warfare states? That is, can Europe afford to spend more on welfare programs because the United States provides most of its military protection?

I care about poverty, but not *relative poverty*. The reason I don't care about relative poverty is because I care about poverty, and relative poverty is not a measure poverty. It means *inequality*, but the label is meant to invoke the moral significance of *poverty*. "Relative poverty" is a trick concept meant to bamboozle an audience, to get them sufficiently confused to start caring about inequality when they meant to care about poverty instead.

To illustrate, according to the OECD, the United States has a "poverty rate" of nearly 20%, higher than Mexico, Turkey, Czechia, and Greece. When I give you that statistic, you might think, wow, Americans are surprisingly poor. But, no, here is how the OECD defines the poverty rate:

> The poverty rate is the ratio of the number of people (in a given age group) whose income falls below the poverty line; *taken as half the median household income of the total population*. It is also available by broad age group: child poverty (0–17 years old), working-age poverty and elderly poverty (66 year-olds or more). *However, two countries with the same poverty rates may differ in terms of the relative income-level of the poor.*[14]

In other words, the "poverty rate" is not a poverty rate, but a measure of income inequality. This definition creates confusion where there could have been clarity. Americans are not poorer than Mexicans—on the contrary, even after adjusting for the higher cost of living in the United States, the mean and median Mexican earns an amount below the US poverty line. Of course, some Mexicans are richer than some Americans, but generally speaking, relatively poor Americans are richer than typical Mexicans.

What if instead of pretending to talk about poverty when we mean inequality, we actually talk about poverty? To do that, we would need to examine just how much income below-average Americans have before receiving welfare state transfers, and then also examine the income and goods and services they receive in-kind from the US welfare state. Economist from *Just Facts* have pointed out that if we use publicly available OECD, World Bank, and US Bureau of Economic Affairs data, then that bottom 20% of American households—the ones the OECD says fall inside the poverty line—consume more goods and services per year than the *average* households in Sweden, Canada, the United Kingdom, Australia, Iceland, and most other OECD countries. They fall just below the Netherlands, Norway, and Italy.[15] To be clear—since I don't want to trick you—that these

[14] https://data.oecd.org/inequality/poverty-rate.htm. Emphasis added.
[15] https://www.justfacts.com/news_poorest_americans_richer_than_europe.

numbers include the consumption funded by and services provided by their respective welfare states. So, it would be misleading and dishonest if I said the US welfare state was useless because poor Americans already are doing better than most average Europeans—one of the reasons they are doing better is that they receive welfare benefits. But it would also be even more misleading if others said that because the US has a 20% "poverty" rate as defined by the OECD, we need to increase taxes and transfers. However, you can easily find people making such misleading and dishonest arguments.

I think we owe the American "poor" something more, something besides *more money*. We should get out of their way and stop hurting them. We could make it easier for them to start a business by reducing or eliminating many zoning and licensing laws. We should reduce regulations on housing and stop NIMBYism, which prevents new construction and makes housing unaffordable. We should improve public education for citizens not on the college preparatory track, perhaps by copying the German system. I haven't spent much time discussing these things in this book because my main concern is to end real poverty, not inequality among the rich and privileged people who live in Western nation-states.

References

Acosta, P., Calderon, C., Fajnzylber, P., and Lopez, H., "What is the Impact of International Remittances on Poverty and Inequality in Latin America?," *World Development* 36 (2008), 89–114.

Adams, Jr., Richard, H., and Page, J., "Do International Migration and Remittances Reduce Poverty in Developing Countries?," *World Development* 33 (2005), 1645–69.

Adler, M., and Holtug, N., "Prioritarianism: A Response to Critics," *Politics, Philosophy, and Economics* 18 (2019), 101–44.

Akerlof, G., "The Economics of 'Tagging' as Applied to the Optimal Income Tax, Welfare Reforms, and Manpower Planning," *American Economic Review* 68 (1978), 8–19.

Alesina, A., and Dollar, D., "Who Gives Foreign Aid to Whom and Why," *Journal of Economic Growth* 5 (2000), 33–53.

Alesina, A., and Glaeser, E., *Fighting Poverty in the U.S. and Europe: A World of Difference*, Oxford: Oxford University Press, 2004.

Alesina, A., Glaeser, E., and Sacerdote, B., "Why Doesn't the US Have a European-Style Welfare State?," *Brookings Papers on Economic Activity* 32 (2001), 187–277.

Alesina, A., and Marco T., "The Political Effects of Immigration: Culture Or Economics?," *Journal of Economic Literature* 62 (2024), 5–46.

Alesina, A., and Rodrik, D., "Distributive Politics and Economic Growth," *Quarterly Journal of Economics* 109 (1994), 465–90.

Anderson, E., "What Is the Point of Equality?," *Ethics* 109 (1999), 287–337.

Arneson, R., "Extreme Cosmopolitanisms Defended," *Critical Review of International Social and Political Philosophy* 19 (2016), 555–73.

Arneson, R., *Prioritarianism*, Cambridge: Cambridge University Press, 2022.

Arneson, R., "Basic Range Equality, Rational Agency Capacity, and Potentiality," in G. Floris and N. Kirby, eds., *How Can We Be Equals? Basic Equality: Its Meaning, Justification, and Scope*, Oxford: Oxford University Press, 2024, 305–24.

Balboni, C., Bandiera, O., Burgess, R. Ghatak, M., and Heil, A., "Why Do People Stay Poor?," *Quarterly Journal of Economics* 137 (2022), 785–844.

Bannerjee, A., and Duflo, E., *Good Economics for Hard Times*, New York: Public Affairs, 2019.

Bartels, L., *Unequal Democracy: The Political Economy of the New Gilded Age*, 2nd ed., Princeton: Princeton University Press, 2018.

Barth, E., Moene, K., and Willumsen, F., "The Scandinavian Model—An Interpretation," *Journal of Public Economics* 117 (2014), 60–72.

Benhabib, S., *The Rights of Others*. New York: Cambridge University Press, 2004.

Bhuller, M., Moene, K., Mogstad, M., and Vestad, O., "Facts and Fantasies about Wage Setting and Collective Bargaining," *Journal of Economic Perspectives* 36 (2022), 29–52.

Bianchi, N., and Paridisi, M., "Countries for Old Men: An Analysis of the Age Pay Gap," NBER working paper 32340, 2024.

Bowles, S., *The New Economics of Inequality and Redistribution*, Cambridge: Cambridge University Press, 2012.

Brennan, J., *Libertarianism: What Everyone Needs to Know*, Oxford: Oxford University Press, 2012.

Brennan, J., *Why It's OK to Want to be Rich*, New York: Routledge Press, 2020.

Brennan, J., "Get a Job and Pay Your Taxes! What Utopophiles Must Say to the Western Poor," *Social Philosophy and Policy* 39 (2022), 48–67.

Brennan, J., *Why Not Capitalism?*, 2nd ed., Routledge Press, 2024.

Brennan, J., and Freiman, C., "Why not Anarchism?" *Politics, Philosophy & Economics* 21 (2022), 415–36.

Browning, M., and Bonke, J., "Allocation within the Household: Direct Survey Evidence," Oxford: Department of Economics, 2006.

Card, D., Kluve, J., and Weber, A., "What Works? A Meta Analysis of Recent Active Labor Market Program Evaluations," *Journal of the European Economic Association* 16 (2018), 894–931.

Case, A., and Deaton, A., *Deaths of Despair and the Future of Capitalism*, Princeton: Princeton University Press, 2021.

Chambers, D., McLaughlin, P. A., and Stanley, L., "Regulation and Poverty: An Empirical Examination of The Relationship Between the Incidence of Federal Regulation and the Occurrence of Poverty Across the US States," *Public Choice* 180 (2019), 131–44.

Chancel, L., et al., eds., *World Inequality Report 2022*, Cambridge, MA: Harvard University Press, 2022.

Clemens, M., "Economics and Immigration: Trillion Dollar Bills on the Sidewalk?," *Journal of Economic Perspectives* 25 (2011), 83–106.

Clemens, M., and Bazzi, S., "Don't Close the Golden Door: Making Immigration Policy Work for Development," in N. Birdsall, ed., *The White House and the World: A Global Development Agenda for the Next U.S. President*, Washington, DC: Center for Global Development, 2008, 241–72.

Cohen, G. A., *Why Not Socialism?* Princeton: Princeton University Press, 2009.

Collier, P., *The Bottom Billion: Why the Poorest Countries Are Failing and What Can Be Done about It*, Oxford: Oxford University Press, 2008.

Collier, P., *Exodus: How Migration Is Changing Our World*, Oxford: Oxford University Press, 2013.

Corneo, G., *Is Capitalism Obsolete: A Journey through Alternative Economic Systems*, Daniel Steuer tr., Cambridge, MA: Harvard University Press, 2017.

Cowen, T., *Stubborn Attachments: A Vision for a Society of Free, Prosperous, and Responsible Individuals*, San Francisco, CA: Stripe Press, 2018.

Dahl, R., *A Preface to Economic Democracy*, Berkeley: University of California Press, 1985.

Dawson, J. W., and Seater, J. J., "Federal Regulation and Aggregate Economic Growth," *Journal of Economic Growth* 12 (2013), 137–77.

Deaton, A., *The Great Escape: Health, Wealth, and the Origins of Inequality*, Princeton and Oxford: Princeton University Press, 2013.

Deaton, A., *Economics in America: An Immigrant Economist Explores the Land of Inequality*, Princeton: Princeton University Press, 2023.

de Haas, H., "International Migration, Remittances and Development: Myths and Facts," *Third World Quarterly* 26 (2005), 1269–84.

de Haas, H., "Migration, Remittances and Regional Development in Southern Morocco," *Geoforum* 37 (2006), 565–80.

DeLong, B., *Macroeconomics*. Columbus: McGraw Hill, 2002.

Desilver, D., "Remittances from Abroad Are Major Economic Assets for Some Developing Countries," *Pew Research Center*, January 29, 2018. http://www.pewresearch.org/fact-tank/2018/01/29/remittances-from-abroad-are-major-economic-assets-for-some-developing-countries/.

Dollar, D., and Kraay, A., "Growth is Good for the Poor," *Journal of Economic Growth* 7 (2002), 195–225.

Dustmann, C., and Frattini, T., "The Fiscal Effects of Immigration to the UK," *Centre for Research and Analysis of Migration*, 2013. http://www.cream-migration.org/publ_uploads/CDP_22_13.pdf.

Easterly, W., *The Elusive Quest for Growth: Economists' Adventures and Misadventures in the Tropics*, Cambridge, MA: MIT Press, 2001.

Ellison, C. G., Shin, H., and Leal, D. L., "The Contact Hypothesis and Attitudes Toward Latinos in the United States," *Social Science Quarterly* 92 (2011), 938–58.

Elster, J., *An Introduction to Karl Marx*, Cambridge: Cambridge University Press, 1986.

Esping-Andersen, G., *The Incomplete Revolution: Adapting to Women's New Roles*, Cambridge, UK: Polity Press, 2009.

Esping-Andersen, G., and Cimentada, J., "Ability and Mobility: The Relative Influence of Skills and Social Origin on Social Mobility," *Social Science Research* 75 (2018), 13–31.

Fletcher, G., *The Philosophy of Well-Being: An Introduction*, Routledge, 2016.

Fleurbaey, M., "Equality versus Priority: How Relevant Is the Distinction?," *Economics and Philosophy* 31 (2015), 203–17.

Fleurbaey, M., et al., *A Manifesto for Social Progress: Ideas for a Better Society*, Cambridge: Cambridge University Press, 2018.

Folbre, N., "Inequality and Time Use in the Household," in W. Salverda, B. Nolan, and T. M. Smeeding, eds., *The Oxford Handbook of Economic Inequality*, Oxford: Oxford University Press, 2009, 342–63.

Frankfurt, H., *Inequality*, Princeton and Oxford: Princeton University Press, 2015.

Fraser, N., "After the Family Wage: Gender Equity and the Welfare State," *Political Theory* 22 (1994), 591–618.

Freiman, C., "The Marginal Cases Argument for Open Immigration," *Public Affairs Quarterly* 29 (2015), 257–75.

Friedberg, R., and Hunt, J., "The Impact of Immigrants on Host Wages," *Journal of Economic Perspectives* 9 (1995), 23–44.

Frølund Thomsen, J. P., "How Does Intergroup Contact Generate Ethnic Tolerance? The Contact Hypothesis in a Scandinavian Context," *Scandinavian Political Studies* 35 (2012), 159–78.

Gihleb, R., Giuntella, O., and Stella, L., "Exposure to Past Immigration Waves and Attitudes Toward Newcomers," *Migration Studies* 10 (2022), 789–814.

Gilens, M., *Why Americans Hate Welfare: Race, Media, and the Politics of Antipoverty Policy,* Chicago and London: University of Chicago Press, 1999.

Gilens, M., *Affluence and Influence: Economic Inequality and Political Power in America,* New York: Russell Sage and Princeton: Princeton University Press, 2012.

Goldin, C, "Babies and the Macroeconomy," Coase lecture, April, 2025.

Gregory, M., "Gender and Economic Inequality," in W. Salverda, B. Nolan, and T. M. Smeeding, eds., *The Oxford Handbook of Economic Inequality*, Oxford: Oxford University Press, 2009, 284–312.

Gupta, S., Pattillo, C. A., and Wagh, S., "Effect of Remittances on Poverty and Financial Development in Sub-Saharan Africa," *World Development* 37 (2009), 104–15.

Gwartney, J., Lawson, R., and Hall, J., *Economic Freedom of the World, 2014 Report.* Vancouver: Fraser Institute, 2015.

Gwartney, J., Lawson, R., and Hall, J., *Economic Freedom of the World, 2016 Report.* Vancouver: Fraser Institute, 2017.

Gwartney, J., Lawson, R., Murphy, R., Abubaker, M., Celico, A., Hammond, A., McMahon, F., and Rode, M., *Economic Freedom of the World: 2023 Annual Report*. Vancouver: Fraser Institute, 2023.

Halliday, D., *The Inheritance of Wealth*. Oxford: Oxford University Press, 2018.

Hanson, G., "The Economic Consequences of the International Migration of Labor," *Annual Review of Economics* 1 (2009), 179–207.

Heckman, J., "Skill Formation and the Economics of Investing in Disadvantaged Children," *Science* 312 (2006), 1900–2.

Heckman, J., and Landerso, R., "Lessons for Americans from Denmark about Inequality and Social Mobility," *Labour Economics* 77 (2022), 1–14.

Helliwell, J., Layard, R., Sachs, J., De Neve, J. A., Aknin, L., and Wang, S., *World Happiness Report 2021*, https://worldhappiness.report. accessed March 1, 2026.

Huemer, M., "Is There a Right to Immigrate?" *Social Theory and Practice* 36 (2010), 429–61.

Huerta, M. et al., "Fathers' Leave and Fathers' Involvement: Evidence from Four OECD Countries," *European Journal of Social Security* 16 (2014), 308–46.

Iyer, R., et al., "Understanding Libertarian Morality: The Psychological Dispositions of Self-Identified Libertarians," *PLoS One* 7 (2012). https://doi.org/10.1371/journal.pone.0042366.

Jensen, C., *Equality in the Nordic World,* Aarhus: Aarhus University Press (along with University of Wisconsin Press), 2021.

Jensen, C., *Welfare,* Baltimore: Johns Hopkins University Press and Aarhus, Aarhus University Press, 2023.

Jensen, C., and van Kersbergen, K., *The Politics of Inequality*, Oxford: Oxford University Press, 2017.

Kenworthy, L., *Progress for the Poor*, Oxford: Oxford University Press, 2011.

Kenworthy, L., *Social Democratic Capitalism*, New York: Oxford University Press, 2020.

Kenworthy, L., *Would Democratic Socialism Be Better?*, New York: Oxford University Press, 2022.

Kerr, S. P., and Kerr, W. R., *Economic Impacts of Immigration: A Survey*. No. w16736. Cambridge, MA: National Bureau of Economic Research, 2011.

Knudsen, A. et al. [Nordic Burden of Disease Collaborators], "Life Expectancy and Disease Burden in the Nordic Countries," *Lancet Public Health* 4 (2019), e658–e669.

Koechlin, V., and Gianmarco, L., "International Remittances and Income Inequality: An Empirical Investigation," *Journal of Economic Policy Reform* 10 (2007), 123–41.

Kogelmann, B., "In Defense of (Limited) Oligarchy," *Public Affairs Quarterly* 37 (2023), 352–70.

Kolodny, N., *The Pecking Order: Social Hierarchy as a Philosophical Problem*, Cambridge, MA: Harvard University Press, 2023.

Krugman, P., "The CPI and the Rat Race," *Slate*, December 22, 1996. http://www.slate.com/articles/business/the_dismal_science/1996/12/the_cpi_and_the_rat_race.html.

Krugman, P., "Something Not Rotten in Denmark," *New York Times*, August 16, 2018.

Landerso, and Heckman, J., "The Scandinavian Fantasy: The Sources of Intergenerational Mobility in Denmark and the US," *Scandinavian Journal of Economics* 119 (2017), 178–230.

Landes, D., *The Wealth and Poverty of Nations: Why Some Are So Rich and Some are So Poor*. New York: W. W. Norton and Co, 1999.

Layard, R., *Happiness*, New York: Penguin Publishing, 2005.

Lindbeck, A., "The Swedish Experiment," *Journal of Economic Literature* 35 (1997), 1273–1319.

Lindert, P., *Growing Public: Social Spending and Economic Growth since the Eighteenth Century*, vol. 1, Cambridge: Cambridge University Press, 2004.

Lindert, P., *Making Social Spending Work*, Cambridge: Cambridge University Press, 2021.

Lindert, P., and Williamson, J., *Unequal Gains: American Growth and Inequality since 1700*, Princeton and Oxford: Princeton University Press, 2016.

Loayza, N. V., Oviedo, A. M., and Serven, L., "The Impact of Regulation on Growth and Informality: Cross-Country Evidence," *Policy Research Working Paper No. 3623*. Washington, DC: World Bank, 2005.

Longhi, S., Nijkamp, P., and Poot, J., "A Meta-Analytic Assessment of the Effect of Immigration on Wages," *Journal of Economic Surveys* 19 (2005), 451–77.

Longhi, S., Nijkamp, P., and Poot, J., "The Impact of Immigration on the Employment of Natives in Regional Labour Markets: A Meta-Analysis," 2006.

Longhi, S., Nijkamp, P., and Poot, J., "Joint Impacts of Immigration on Wages and Employment: Review and Meta-Analysis," *Journal of Geographical Systems* 12 (2010), 355–87.

López-Córdova, E., Tokman, A., and Verhoogen, E., "Globalization, Migration, and Development: The Role of Mexican Migrant Remittances," *Economía* 6 (2005), 217–56.

Macedo, S., "The Moral Dilemma of US Immigration Policy: Open Borders versus Social Justice," in C. M. Swain, ed., *Debating Immigration*, New York: Cambridge University Press, 2007, 63–82.

Mackenbach, J., *Health Inequalities: Persistence and Change in European Welfare States*, Oxford: Oxford University Press, 2019.

Maddison, A., *Contours of the World Economy, 1-2030 AD: Essays in Macro-Economic History*. New York: Oxford University Press, 2007.

Maldonado, L., and Niewenhuis, R., "Family Policies and Single-Parent Poverty in 18 OECD Countries 1978–2008," Luxembourg Income Study working paper series No. 622, 2014.

Marx, K., McLellan, D., ed., *Karl Marx: Selected Readings*, Oxford: Oxford University Press, 1977.

McKenzie, D., and Rapoport, H., "Network Effects and the Dynamics of Migration and Inequality: Theory and Evidence From Mexico," *Journal of Development Economics* 84 (2008), 1–24.

Milanovic, B., *Worlds Apart: Measuring International and Global Inequality*. Princeton: Princeton University Press, 2007.

Milanovic, B., *Capitalism Alone: The Future of the System That Rules the World*, Cambridge, MA: Harvard University Press, 2019.

Mill, J. S., "The Probable Futurity of the Labouring Classes," in *Principles of Political Economy*, Bk. 4, ch. 7, originally published 1848; *On Liberty*, 1859; *Utilitarianism*, 1861, *The Subjection of Women, 1869*, all available at https://oll.libertyfund.org/titles/mill-the-collected-works-of-john-stuart-mill-volume-iii-principles-of-political-economy-part-ii, accessed March 3, 2026.

Miller, D., *Principles of Social Justice*. Cambridge, MA: Harvard University Press, 2001.

Miller, D., *Strangers in Our Midst*, Cambridge MA: Harvard University Press, 2018.

Miller, T., Kim, A., and Robert, J. *2019 Index of Economic Freedom*. Washington, DC: Heritage Institute, 2019.

Moene, K., and Wallerstein, M., "Inequality, Social Insurance, and Redistribution," *American Political Science Review* 95 (2001), 859–74.

Mogstad, M., Salvanes, K., and Torsvik, G., "Income Inequality in the Nordic Countries: Facts, Myths, and Lessons," 2025, http://www.nber.org/papers/w33444, accessed March 1, 2026.

Mueller, D., *Public Choice III*, New York: Cambridge University Press, 2003.

Mullainathan, S., and Shafir, S., *Scarcity: Why Having Too Little Means So Much*, New York: Henry Holt and Co., 2013.

Murphy, L., and Nagel, T., *The Myth of Ownership*, Oxford: Oxford University Press, 2002.

Nair, G., "Misperceptions of Relative Affluence and Support for International Redistribution," *Journal of Politics* 80 (2018), 815–30.

Nowrasteh, A., and Cole, S., "Building a Wall Around the Welfare State, Instead of the Country," *Cato Institute Policy Analysis* #732, July 25, 2013. http://www.cato.org/publications/policy-analysis/building-wall-around-welfare-state-instead-country.

Nozick, R., *Anarchy, State, and Utopia*, New York: Basic Books, 1974.

OECD, "The Fiscal Impact of Immigration in OECD Countries," in *OECD, International Migration Outlook 2013*, Paris: ECD Publishing, 2013. http://dx.doi.org/10.1787/migr_outlook-2013-6-en.

OECD, *Reporting Gender Pay Gaps in OECD Countries,* Paris: OECD Publishing, 2023 https://doi.org/10.1787/ea13aa68-en.

Okkerse, L., "How to Measure Labour Market Effect of Immigration: A Review," *Journal of Economic Surveys* 22 (2008), 1–30.

Ottaviano, G., and Giovanni, P., "Rethinking the Effect of Immigration on Wages," *Journal of the European Economic Association* 10.1 (2012), 152–97.

Ottaviano, G., and Peri, G., *Immigration and National Wages: Clarifying the Theory and the Empirics*. No. w14188. Cambridge, MA: National Bureau of Economic Research, 2008.

Page, B., and Gilens, M., *Democracy in America: What Has Gone Wrong and What We Can Do about It*, Chicago: University of Chicago Press, 2017.

Parfit, D., "Equality or Priority?" *The Lindley Lectures*. Kansas: University of Kansas Press, 1991.

Pearson, J., "Realism in the Ethics of Immigration," *Philosophy and Social Criticism* 49 (2023), 950–74.

Peri, G., and Sparber, C., "Task Specialization, Immigration, and Wages," *American Economic Journal: Applied Economics* 1 (2009), 135–69.

Petts, R., and Knoester, C., "Paternity Leave-Taking and Father Engagement," *Journal of Marriage and Family* 80 (2018), 1142–62.

Phelps, G., and Crabtree, S., "Worldwide, Mean Household Income about $10,000," *Gallup*, December 16, 2013. https://news.gallup.com/poll/166211/worldwide-median-household-income-000.aspx.

Pinker, S., *The Better Angels of Our Nature: Why Violence Has Declined*, New York: Viking Penguin, 2011.

Pritchett, L., *Let Their People Come: Breaking the Gridlock on International Labor Mobility*. Washington, DC: Center for Global Development, 2006.

Pritchett, L., "The Cliff at the Border," in R. Kanbur and M. Spence, eds., *Equity and Growth in a Changing World*, Washington, DC: World Bank, 2010, 263–86.

Putnam, R., "*E Pluribus Unum:* Diversity and Community in the Twenty-First Century," *Scandinavian Political Studies* 30 (2007), 137–74.

Quigley, J. M., and Raphael, S., "Regulation and the High Cost of Housing in California," *American Economic Review* 95 (2005), 323–28.

Rawls, J., *A Theory of Justice,* rev. ed., Cambridge, MA: Harvard University Press, 1999a.

Rawls, J., *The Law of Peoples*, Cambridge, MA: Harvard University Press, 1999b.

Rawls, J., and Kelly, E., ed., *Justice as Fairness: A Restatement*, Cambridge, MA: Harvard University Press, 2001.

Roemer, J., "Should Marxists Be Interested in Exploitation?," *Philosophy and Public Affairs* 14 (1985), 30–65.

Rothstein, B., *Just Institutions Matter: The Moral and Political Logic of the Universal Welfare State*, Cambridge: Cambridge University Press, 1998.

Saez, E., and Zucman, G., *The Triumph of Injustice: How the Rich Dodge Taxes and How to Make Them Pay*, New York: W. W. Norton and Co., 2019.

Sangiovanni, A., "Global Justice, Reciprocity, and the State," *Philosophy and Public Affairs* 35 (2007), 3–39.

Schall, C., *The Rise and Fall of the Miraculous Welfare Machine: Immigration and Social Democracy in Twentieth Century Sweden*, Ithaca and London: ILR Press, 2016.

Scheffler, S., "What Is Egalitarianism?," *Philosophy and Public Affairs* 31 (2003), 5–39.

Schmidtz, D., and Brennan, J., *A Brief History of Liberty*. Malden, MA: Wiley-Blackwell, 2010.

Sejersted, F., Daly, R., tr., Adams, M., ed. *The Age of Social Democracy: Norway and Sweden in the Twentieth Century*, Princeton: Princeton University Press, 2011.

Shafir, E., "Decisions in Poverty Contexts," *Social Cognition* 18 (2017), 131–6.

Smith, A., *An Inquiry Into the Nature and Causes of the Wealth of Nations*. London: Methuen and Co., 1904 [1776]. http://www.econlib.org/library/Smith/smWN.html#.

Stark, O., Edward, T., and Yitzhaki, S., "Remittances and Inequality," *The Economic Journal* 96 (1986), 722–40.

Stringham, E., *Private Governance*. New York: Oxford University Press, 2015.

Surprenant, C., and Brennan, J., *Injustice For All*, New York: Routledge Press, 2020.

Taylor, E. J., "The New Economics of Labour Migration and the Role of Remittances in the Migration Process," *International Migration* 37 (1999), 63–88.

Thomas, D. W., "Regressive Effects of Regulation," *Public Choice* 180 (2019), 1–10.

Vrousalis, N., *Exploitation as Domination: What Makes Capitalism Unjust*, Oxford: Oxford University Press, 2023.

Waldfogel, J., *What Children Need*, Cambridge, MA: Harvard University Press, 2006.

Walzer, M., *Spheres of Justice: A Defense of Pluralism and Equality*. New York: Basic Books, 1983.

Weil, D., *Economic Growth*, 3rd ed., New York: Pearson, 2013.

Wellman, C., "Immigration and Freedom of Association," *Ethics* 119 (2008), 109–41.

Weyl, G., "The Openness-Equality Tradeoff in Global Redistribution," *Economic Journal* 28 (2018), F1–F36.

World Economic Forum, *Global Gender Report 2020*. Geneva, Switzerland, 2019.

Yglesias, M., "Denmark's Prime Minister Says Bernie Sanders Is Wrong to Call His Country Socialist," *Vox*, October 31, 2015. https://www.vox.com/2015/10/31/9650030/denmark-prime-minister-bernie-sanders.

Index

For the benefit of digital users, indexed terms that span two pages (e.g., 52–53) may, on occasion, appear on only one of those pages.

Note: Bold page numbers indicate an overarching discussion.

Tables and figures are indicated by an italic *t* and *f* following the page number.